HUMOR
OF A
COUNTRY
LAWYER

Sam J. Ervin, Jr.

HUMOR OF A COUNTRY LAWYER

University of North Carolina Press

Chapel Hill and London

Library of Congress Cataloging in Publication Data
Ervin, Sam J. (Sam James), 1896–1985
Humor of a country lawyer.
Includes index.
1. Ervin, Sam J. (Sam James), 1896–1985—Anecdotes.
2. North Carolina—Politics and government—Anecdotes,
facetiae, satire, etc. 3. United States—Politics and
government—1945–   —Anecdotes, facetiae, satire,
etc. 4. Legislators—United States—Biography—
Anecdotes, facetiae, satire, etc. 5. United States.
Congress. Senate—Biography—Anecdotes, facetiae,
satire, etc. I. Title.
E748.E93A34 1983   328.73′092′4   83-7045
ISBN 0-8078-1566-7 (cloth)
ISBN 0-8078-4464-0 (pbk.)

Photograph by Ann Hawthorne

*I dedicate this book
with love and laughter to
Miss Margaret's children and mine,
Judge Sam J. Ervin III,
Leslie Ervin Hansler, and
Laura Ervin Smith.*

Contents

Preface

When I decided to write a book on humor, I made these resolves: to ignore everything everybody else had written on humor; to exclude stories I had found in books; to include stories that had been orally communicated to me by others, or that had been incident to events in which I had participated, or that had been incident to events observed by me as a bystander; and to excommunicate dirty jokes and stories begotten by an obsession with sex.

I have faithfully adhered to these resolves except the one relating to stories found in books. I violated it once. Despite the limitations they have imposed upon me, I hope that my readers, if I should be so fortunate as to have any, will find something in these pages to make their hearts merry.

To borrow a Shakespearean phrase, this is a consummation devoutly to be wished. As Proverbs 17:22 attests, "A merry heart doeth good like a medicine."

Unfortunately, humor has always been in low repute among people whose over-serious minds ban it from their hearts. This is true nowadays of misanthropes who multiply their miseries by decrying the therapeutic potency of humor and by refusing to take dosages of it for their pessimism. They equate humor with buffoonery and allege that its devotees are silly fools unconcerned with the problems that bedevil humanity. I defy the misanthropes, and deny their allegation.

Humor is one of God's most marvelous gifts. Humor gives us smiles, laughter, and gaiety. Humor reveals the roses and hides the thorns. Humor makes our heavy burdens light and smooths the rough spots in our pathways. Humor endows us with the capacity to clarify the obscure, to simplify the complex, to deflate the pompous, to chastise the arrogant, to point a moral, and to adorn a tale.

Humor answers the ancient outcry, "Is there no balm in Gilead? Is there no physician there?" Humor binds up the wounds of those who suffer, wipes the tears from the eyes of those who weep, and heals the hurts of those whose hearts are broken.

I take more space to narrate humorous stories than the authors of most standard collections of anecdotes assign to them. The hearer or reader loses much of the flavor of a humorous story unless he knows the circumstances that gave it birth.

I entitle this book *Humor of a Country Lawyer*. For some time before Watergate, I was accustomed to refer to myself as an old country lawyer. This sobriquet has been adopted by some of my countrymen following an incident in the Senate Select Committee's investigation of that tragic episode of our nation's history. The incident occurred as I ended my questioning of former secretary of commerce Maurice Stans, a somewhat reluctant witness, who served as Finance Chairman of Nixon's reelection committee, and stored substantial sums of campaign funds in cash in safes controlled by him.

The Watergate burglary and bugging were financed with moneys that Hugh W. Sloan, Jr., the committee treasurer, acting with Stans's authority, took from these safes and gave to G. Gordon Liddy, the committee's legal adviser, who masterminded the burglary and bugging.

Stans vehemently asserted he had no knowledge or information or suspicion that Liddy was going to use the moneys for any illegal purpose, and that he knew nothing about the Watergate affair except what he learned from the news media after its perpetration.

I questioned Stans with vigor concerning his testimony, and thus irritated Senator Edward J. Gurney, a member of the committee, who uttered this protest: "I for one have not appreciated the harassment of this witness by the chairman in the questioning that has just ended. I think this Senate committee ought to act in fairness."

As a practitioner of the biblical admonition "a soft answer turneth away wrath," I said: "I have asked the witness questions to find out what the truth is. I am sorry my distinguished friend from Florida does not approve of my method of examining the witness. I am an old country lawyer, and I don't know the finer ways to do it. I just have to do it my way."

Lyndon Johnson once said to me, "When I see a country lawyer approaching, I grab my pocketbook, and run." I replied, "That's not surprising. Country lawyers often compel evil-doers to disgorge their ill-gotten gains."

Country lawyers have some advantages their more prestigious city brethren do not enjoy. Their clients come to them from all classes and conditions of men. They take their cases, civil or criminal, great or small, and learn to appraise aright their joys and their sorrows.

I am grateful to four persons for aiding me in producing this book. They are Mary B. McBryde, my secretary, who deciphered the obscure words I scribbled with pencils on yellow tablets, and converted them into a legible manuscript; Leslie Ervin Hansler, my daughter, who read parts of the manuscript and made helpful comments on them; David Perry, my editor, whose wise advice enabled me to improve the manuscript in both form and content; and Margaret Bell Ervin, my wife of fifty-eight years, who extended to me her never-failing patience and encouragement.

Acknowledgments

I acknowledge my deep gratitude to the following for permission to use previously published and copyrighted materials: William E. Anderson, of Raleigh, North Carolina, executor of the estate of Thad Stem, Jr., and Mrs. Marguerite L. Stem, of Oxford, North Carolina, widow of Thad Stem, Jr., for permission to use materials communicated by me to Thad Stem, Jr., and Alan Butler which they used in the book *Senator Sam Ervin's Best Stories* (Durham: Moore, 1973); Scripture Press Publications, Ltd., of Toronto, Canada, for permission to quote Annie Johnson Flint's poem "What God Hath Promised"; Arthur P. Laws, of Atlanta, Georgia, for permission to use the two anecdotes that appeared in the book of his grandfather, Judge Arthur G. Powell, entitled *I Can Go Home Again*; Miss Alba R. Malone, of Arlington, Virginia, for permission to quote the poem "To A Judge," written by her uncle, Judge Walter Malone, of Memphis, Tennessee; the North Carolina Division of Archives and History for permission to use material which appeared in my article "Humor, Wise and Otherwise" in the Spring 1982 issue of the *North Carolina Historical Review*; and Frank Lebby Stanton III, of Trussville, Alabama, for permission to quote the poem "This World We're Living In," written by his grandfather, Frank Lebby Stanton.

With the oral consent of Random House, its publisher, I have used in the chapter "Humor in the Watergate Investigation" some material similar to that appearing in my book *The Whole Truth: The Watergate Conspiracy* (1980), which is copyrighted by me.

HUMOR OF A COUNTRY LAWYER

Chapter 1

The Nature and Uses of Humor

❦ ❦ ❦

The dictionary defines humor as the faculty of perceiving the amusing or comical. This definition falls short of describing humor at its best. Humor at its best is the faculty of perceiving wisdom and communicating it in amusing or comical ways which command attention.

It has been truthfully said that the world has joked incessantly for over fifty centuries. Its action in so doing is the only convincing evidence we have of the superiority of man over earth's other creatures, to whom the Lord has denied the capacity to laugh.

Humor exhibits itself most deftly as irony. Clyde R. Hoey, who served North Carolina as governor and senator and was the state's most gifted Democratic orator in his heyday, was a master of irony. When he excoriated a national Republican administration, he asserted, "The Republicans have made their bed; let them lie in it. I for one do not propose to let them lie out of it." When he extolled a North Carolina Democratic administration for its achievements in public health, he declared that the Democrats had increased longevity in the state and made it possible for a Wilkes County Republican to live ten years longer than he should.

Despite my admiration for irony, I find anecdotal humor more understandable. I do not affirm that the effective telling of a humorous story is a science. But I do maintain that it is an art.

The explanation for each of us is to be discovered in large measure in our experiences. Alfred Lord Tennyson so averred in attributing these words to his character Ulysses: "I am a part of all that I have met."

My love for humorous stories originated in my childhood. I was entranced by my father's narration of them. My early days at the bar only intensified this love. I accompanied my father to Bakersville, Boone, and Newland, aided him in trying cases in the superior courts of Mitchell, Watauga, and Avery counties, and received the benefit of the experience of a legal circuit rider.

Owing to the inadequacy of the roads, travel was difficult. If a lawyer residing in Morganton, for example, attended a session of the superior court at Newland, about forty miles away, he took a train in Morganton early Sunday morning and rode to Marion, where he lunched and caught a train for Johnson City, Tennessee. After spending the night in Johnson City, he completed his journey to Newland on the narrow-gauged train now famous as "Tweetsie," in Blowing Rock.

The difficulty of travel to those places compelled the presiding judge and visiting lawyers to remain there as long as the superior court was in session. They spent the evenings swapping humorous stories.

Ordinarily, humor is an instantaneous and spontaneous reaction to an event. Sometimes, however, persons undertake to manufacture what they conceive to be humor.

For the good of my soul, I confess a recent attempt to do this. Inasmuch as I was unable to find a suitable story for the purpose, I devised one to chide United States Supreme Court justices for seeking to convert the court from a judicial tribunal in a government of laws into a judicial oligarchy.

A missionary who had labored mightily for the Lord on earth died. As he neared heaven, Saint Peter flung open the pearly gates and welcomed him warmly to his new home. Saint Peter told the missionary he would grant him any special privilege he craved to manifest heaven's appreciation of his earthly labor. The missionary asked Saint Peter for a conference with the Lord. Saint Peter replied, "Your request is granted, but the conference will have to be delayed until the Lord recovers from His present melancholy. The Lord is disconsolate nowadays because He is unhappy with His limited powers as the Almighty and longs for the jurisdiction of a United States Supreme Court justice."

🦌   Since it is ordinarily an instantaneous reaction to an event, humor is often without conscious objectives. For example, a client visited my law office and told me he wanted to divorce his wife because she talked all the time. When I asked him what she talked about, he replied, "She don't say."

🦌   When they employ humor to achieve objectives, men do so to amuse, to reveal, to convince, to chide, to ridicule, or to alleviate tensions, burdens, or woes.

Although humor can be found in all human activities, it is encountered most frequently in judicial proceedings, legislative assemblies, and political campaigns. It even invades the sacred precincts of religion.

As trial lawyer, politician, and legislator, I recognized the pragmatic value of humor. An ounce of revealing humor often has more power to reveal, convince, or ridicule than do many tons of erudite argument.

In opposing in the North Carolina Legislature of 1925 a proposal to prohibit the teaching of evolution in state colleges and schools, I employed ridicule. I made an observation to this effect: "I confess with reluctance that the passage of this proposal would do good in one respect. It would give joy to the monkeys in the jungle for the North Carolina Legislature to absolve them from responsibility for the conduct of the human race in general and the North Carolina Legislature in particular."

🦌   Artemus Ward, Josh Billings, Mark Twain, George Ade, and Will Rogers are preeminent among American humorists. Our nation is indebted to them for many amusing or comical bits of wisdom.

Artemus Ward: "The Puritans nobly fled from a land of despotism to a land of freedom,where they could not only enjoy their own religion, but could prevent everybody else from enjoyin his."

George Ade: "In uplifting, get underneath." "He had been kicked in the head by a mule when young and believed everything he read in the Sunday papers." "If it were not for the presents, an elopement would be preferable."

Josh Billings: "A sekret ceases tew be a sekret if it iz once confided—it iz like a dollar bill, once broken, it iz never a dollar again." "Love iz like the meazles; we kant have it bad but onst, and the later in life we have it the tuffer it goes with us." "As scarce as truth is, the supply has always been in excess of the demand." "It is better to know nothing than to know what ain't so."

Mark Twain: "Work consists of whatever a body is obliged to do. . . . Play consists of whatever a body is not obliged to do." "A baby is an inestimable blessing and a bother." "When angry, count four; when very angry, swear." "If you pick up a starving dog and make him prosperous, he will not bite you. This is the principal difference between a dog and a man."

Will Rogers: "Everything is funny as long as it is happening to somebody else." "A comedian can only last until he either takes himself serious or his audience takes him serious." "Politics has got so expensive that it takes lots of money to even get beat with."

ℰ North Carolinians have always loved to laugh. Their own merry hearts and the many humorists abiding among them have enabled them to indulge this love. Some of these humorists have had state-wide standings as raconteurs. The talents of some others have been unknown outside the localities in which they lived.

Like other comparisons, an attempt to classify human beings is odious. I, nevertheless, assert with confidence that these Tar Heels have had statewide reputations for recounting stories and anecdotes with skill and wit: Zebulon Baird Vance, Civil War governor and senator; James M. Leach, lawyer and politician of Lexington; Robert Laban Abernethy, Methodist minister and president of Rutherford College; William C. Newland, Democratic warhorse of Caldwell County; Moses N. Harshaw, Republican exhorter of Caldwell County; Gus Self, eloquent and fearless attorney of Catawba County; Burgess S. Crisp, state legislator of Dare County; Tom Bost and Nell Battle Lewis, journalists of Raleigh; Walter P. Stacy, chief justice of North Carolina; Walter D. Siler, lawyer and jurist of Chatham County; Thad Eure, long-time secretary of state; and Chub Seawell, the captivating wit of Moore County.

Zeb Vance, the state's most beloved son, was also one of the nation's most gifted raconteurs. When Vance was chosen senator, Yankee General Kilpatrick, of Pennsylvania, stated in a letter to the *New York World* that at the end of the Civil War he had captured Vance and made him ride two hundred miles on the bare back of a mule.

Vance sent a letter to the *World* in which he stated that Kilpatrick had knowingly lied. He had surrendered on May 2, 1865, to General Scholfield, who had kindly permitted him to await further events at his home in Statesville; he was re-arrested at Statesville on May 13, 1865, by Major Porter, who extended to him nothing but courtesy, and conveyed him by buggy and train to General Kilpatrick's headquarters; and he never saw a mule during the entire trip, but on his arrival at General Kilpatrick's headquarters "thought he saw an ass." Vance closed his letter by affirming that subsequent events had confirmed that opinion.

❦ Judge Siler authored many witticisms. One of them had as its target the understandable habit of Josephus Daniels, the famous publisher of the Raleigh *News and Observer*, to mention with frequency his fine service as secretary of the navy under President Woodrow Wilson.

A member of the North Carolina Legislature whose pride in the state knew no bounds undertook to end any doubt in respect to the authenticity of the Mecklenburg Declaration of Independence. To this end, he introduced a resolution affirming that the patriots of Mecklenburg County really did meet in convention at Charlotte on May 20, 1775, and declare themselves to be independent of tyrannical King George III.

The resolution inspired Judge Siler to comment: "If this Legislature is going to determine historical truth by legislative fiat rather than by research, I'm going to insist that it pass a law declaring that Josephus Daniels was in fact Secretary of the Navy during Woodrow Wilson's administration. Josephus has told that so often, nobody believes it anymore."

❦ Walter P. Stacy, North Carolina's greatest of many great jurists, was the son of a circuit-riding Methodist minister who held pastorates in many areas of the state. He won his original nomination for a seat on the North Carolina Supreme Court in 1920 by defeating Judge Benjamin F. Long and other candidates in the Democratic primary. During the campaign preceding the primary, Stacy's enthusiastic supporters in each of the counties in which his father had preached succumbed to the temptation to claim that Stacy had been born in the county.

Judge Long, who was one of the stalwart superior court judges in my early days at the bar, made this trenchant comment after the primary: "I should have had sufficient intelligence to comprehend I couldn't win over an adversary who was born in fifty of North Carolina's one hundred counties."

❧   Chief Justice Stacy was one of my heroes. I had the infinite privilege of serving for a time with him on the North Carolina Supreme Court before my years in the Senate. One cannot appraise too highly the excellence of the contributions he made to civil and criminal justice during the thirty years he adorned the Supreme Court. His powerful and intellectually honest mind was never wearied by his incessant judicial labors. Even when he was confined by serious illness to the hospital, as he often was in his last days, he carried a full share of the court's heavy burdens.

Judge Stacy entertained the abiding conviction that the law is destitute of value as a rule for the conduct of men unless it is stable and uniform as well as just in its operation, and unless it is ascertainable with reasonable certainty within a reasonable time. He was inseparably wedded to the constitutional principle that it is the function of the legislature to make laws and the duty of the judge to interpret and apply them, and would not twist legal precepts either to satisfy his own notions as to what the law ought to be or to please the transitory moods of society.

In defining the bedrock requirements of any system of justice worthy of the name, Judge Stacy said, "A fair jury in jury cases and an impartial judge in all cases are the prime requisites of due process. It is important that the judgments of the court should be respected. To insure this, however, the court must first make sure that they merit respect."

Judge Stacy possessed a profound understanding of history and literature as well as of the law. He was a master of the use of meaningful words, and his opinions abound with unforgettable phrases. For example, in *State* versus *Beal* he said: "It would be almost unbelievable, if history did not record the tragic fact that men have gone to war and cut each other's throats because they could not agree as to what was to become of them after their throats were cut"; and "for some reason, too deep to fathom, men contend more furiously over the road to heaven, which they cannot see, than over their visible walks on earth."

In *State* versus *Wingler* a man whose wife had been brutally slain twenty-nine years before was charged with the murder. Upon his conviction, he appealed the sentence, and Judge Stacy wrote an opinion of unsurpassed pathos and power affirming it. In adjudging that no error appeared in the record "except the great error of the defendant in murdering his wife," Judge Stacy declared, "Though justice sometimes treads with leaden feet, if need be, she strikes with an iron hand. Verily, the wages of sin is death, and sin pays its wages."

The law never had a servant more faithful than Judge Stacy. The bench, the bar, and the people of North Carolina revered him. Despite his manifold virtues, Judge Stacy undertook to practice one deceit upon his fellowman. He tried to hide his humorous heart behind his somewhat stern countenance. But truth will out, and Judge Stacy's secret was betrayed from time to time by his irrepressible sense of humor.

This observation finds apt illustration in his colloquy with Marshall Bell, who practiced law at Murphy, the county seat of Cherokee County, North Carolina's westernmost county.

Bell was retained to perform the legal services necessary to effect a sale of a lot in Murphy which a generous donor had undertaken to give to his church. When he examined the title deed, Bell discovered to his consternation that instead of transferring the lot to the church or to trustees of the church, the deed conveyed the lot to "God Almighty, his heirs and assigns in fee simple."

Shortly after this discovery Bell encountered Judge Stacy on

Fayetteville Street in Raleigh, told him about his discovery, and confessed his inability to fathom the legal steps necessary to consummate the sale.

With a grin on his face and a twinkle in his eye, Judge Stacy assured him, "Brother Bell, you have a simple legal remedy for your problem. All you've got to do is to bring a suit against God Almighty in the superior court of Cherokee County to quiet title to the lot, show by affidavit to the satisfaction of the court that God Almighty cannot be found in Cherokee County, and serve him with summons by publication."

❧   Some of the most intriguing anecdotes are of unknown origin. This is true of one of my favorites, the one about John and his wife, Mandy, who lived in a cabin in the North Carolina mountains west of Asheville.

John and Mandy had always longed for a chiming grandfather clock. After their last child had married and left them, John and Mandy pooled his earnings from occasional runs of his still and her butter and egg money and bought a chiming grandfather clock, which they installed in their cabin.

On the first night after this event they sat up all night and listened to the clock chime because they agreed that it struck "so pretty" it would be a shame for it to strike and for nobody to be awake to hear it.

On the second night they agreed that Mandy would sleep and John would stay awake and listen to the clock strike.

Everything went according to plan until the clock struck 12. Then things went haywire. The clock struck, 13, 14, 15, 16, 17, and 18 in rapid succession. John roused Mandy from her slumber and exclaimed, "Mandy, we've got to do something quick. It's later than I've ever knowed it to be."

❧   What I say about humor is laden with anecdotes having their origin in North Carolina. This is inevitable. North Carolina is the most joyous spot on earth and abounds with humorous stories. I sing without apology and with pride Chapel Hill's favorite song: "I'm a Tar Heel born, I'm a Tar Heel bred, and when I die I'll be a Tar Heel dead."

In my honest and unbiased judgment, the Good Lord will place the Garden of Eden in North Carolina when He restores it to earth. He will do this because He will have so few changes to make in order to achieve perfection.

A girl who was seeking a master's degree in the humanities at Oberlin College visited my senatorial office, informed me she was writing a thesis on Congress, and made many inquiries of me about the Senate and senators.

She asked me what I did to ascertain how my constituents wanted me to vote on issues. I confessed I made no inquiries and conducted no polls to determine their views, but, on the contrary, emulated my kinsman Chief Justice William Alexander Hoke, of the North Carolina Supreme Court, in making my decisions. Judge Hoke said, "When I want to know what the people of North Carolina think, I go to my office, shut the door, sit down at my desk, and consult myself."

In assuring my inquisitor that my mode of operation was not as strange as it might appear to her at first blush, I said, "Some of my people have lived in North Carolina for generations. As a general rule, North Carolinians are a homogenous people descended from ancestors who came to America before the Revolution, and assisted in the founding of the Republic. They differ little in their views concerning fundamental constitutional and governmental principles. I was born and educated in North Carolina. I have lived among North Carolinians all my life. I think like most of them think. When I vote in accordance with my convictions, my votes are pleasing to the overwhelming majority of them."

I confessed to her, however, that I fortified my standing with my constituents with this threat: "If you defeat me, I'm not going to stay in Washington like so many defeated senators and representatives do. I'm coming straight back to North Carolina, and you'll have to put up with me in person."

My record and this threat induced North Carolinians to keep me in the Senate until I voluntarily retired after twenty years' service. During this time I encountered no serious opposition, had no campaign manager, and solicited no political contribution for myself. Although I had been a Democrat all my life and always ran on the Democratic ticket, I was not a bitter partisan, and the Republicans always treated me with kindness. My gratitude to North Carolinians for their support and encouragement knows no bounds.

❧   Insofar as it is employed to relieve tensions, lighten burdens, or alleviate woes, humor has a worth to troubled or sorrowful human beings which far transcends the fabled wealth of Croesus. It is an alchemy which transmutes troubles or sorrows into golden memories.

Frank L. Stanton, a journalist on the staff of the *Atlanta Constitution* many years ago, sensed this truth respecting humor, and epitomized it in this verse.

> This world that we're a-living in,
> Is mighty hard to beat;
> You git a thorn with every rose,
> But ain't the roses sweet.

❧   It is miraculous what humor can do for an individual or a people in moments of distress.

When Congress authorized each state to enshrine in Statuary Hall in the nation's Capitol the statues of her two most useful departed sons or daughters, North Carolinians instinctively and unanimously made Zeb Vance their first choice for this rare honor. They knew that Vance had been a brave soldier, a gifted orator, and a wise statesman. But they did not place his statue in the nation's Parthenon because of his gallantry as a soldier, his eloquence as an orator, or his skill in statecraft. They accorded him this honor because he had laughed his way into their hearts, giving them hope in the dark days of the Civil War and raising their spirits in the darker days of Reconstruction.

Chapter 2

Humor in Burke County

ම් ම් ම්

Humorists lived in all areas of North Carolina, but they were undoubtedly more numerous and gifted in my home county of Burke than elsewhere. Doubting Thomases should understand that my attitude toward Burke County owes more to that entertained by my late friend Arthur Talmadge Abernethy than to my fidelity to truth.

Arthur Talmadge Abernethy persuaded a Mrs. Balfour, who suffered virulent attacks of asthma in the bleak North, to remove thence to Burke County and establish her home on land he sold her. Subsequently, she alleged in a suit against him in Burke County Superior Court that he had induced her to make the purchase and establish her home in Burke County by an assurance which had proved itself to be slightly lacking in veracity, namely, that asthma was unknown in healthy Burke County and that if she settled in Burke she would suffer no more asthmatic attacks. On cross-examination, Mrs. Balfour's lawyer asked Arthur Talmadge how he could justify this assurance. As a loyal son of Burke, he calmly replied, "It's impossible for anybody to say anything too good about Burke County."

Among the myriad raconteurs who have called Burke County home were Joe Allman, Sheriff Alexander Duckworth, Karlton Giles, Bob Hennessee, Joshua Hawkins, Lum Garrison, Isaac T. Avery, Arthur Talmadge Abernethy, Dr. Edward W. Phifer, Francis Garrou, Jim Wilson, Ned Claywell, Russell Berry, Howell J. Hatcher, and Dr. Edward W. Phifer, Jr.

Howell J. Hatcher, who was known as "Doggie" because of the tenacity he displayed playing football at Duke University, served with me in the North Carolina National Guard. He rose to the rank of colonel during the Second World War, commanded the North Carolina State Highway Patrol after his return from service, and was subsequently brevetted a brigadier general in the North Carolina National Guard. He ended his career, as he had begun it, practicing law in Morganton.

Sheriff Alex Duckworth's humor was sometimes caustic. He was wont to select as its targets the great or the near great.

As he was standing on the sidewalk of Union Street in Morganton one Sunday morning, Charles F. McKesson, a distinguished member of the bar, who had been reared a Presbyterian, passed by on his way to Grace Episcopal Church with his Episcopalian wife, and John Gray Bynum, a superior court judge, who had been reared an Episcopalian, passed by en route to the First Presbyterian Church with his Presbyterian wife. The old sheriff thereupon affirmed, "That's the only trade I ever knew where both sides got cheated."

Arthur Talmadge Abernethy was a teller of tall tales. According to him, an old South Mountaineer residing a few miles south of Connelly Springs had reached the age of 125 years. The Barnum and Bailey Circus learned of the event and sent an agent by train to Connelly Springs with a proposed written contract in his pocket providing that the circus would pay the old mountaineer a fancy salary to travel with it and be exhibited to its patrons as the oldest man on earth.

On arrival at Connelly Springs, the agent traveled by buggy over muddy roads to the old mountaineer's home and presented Barnum and Bailey's offer to him. The old mountaineer informed the agent that he was pleased with the offer and was inclined to accept it. Despite repeated entreaties of the agent, however, he refused to sign the proposed contract embodying the offer and told the agent he would not even consider doing so before the next day.

The agent told the old mountaineer, "You surprise me. You tell me that you're pleased with the offer, but that you won't even consider accepting it before tomorrow. Why are you determined to postpone your decision until tomorrow?"

"That's an embarrassing question," the old mountaineer replied, "but I'll answer it. I want to consult my father. I've made it a practice all my life never to enter into any transaction without getting my father's advice."

The agent exclaimed, "You're 125 years old, and you tell me your father's living?" The old mountaineer said, "Yes." The agent inquired, "Where is he?" The old mountaineer responded, "He's gone up the creek to see Grandpa. Grandpa's been ailing lately."

❦ Bob Hennessee was Burke County's most cross-eyed resident with the exception of Sheriff Manly McDowell, who was equally as cross-eyed. As they were walking along Union Street in Morganton in opposite directions, they bumped into each other. Sheriff McDowell inquired, "Bob Hennessee, why in the hell don't you look where you're going?" Hennessee responded, "It wouldn't do a damned bit of good, Manly, because you don't go where you're looking."

❦ Francis Garrou, who was the superintendent of the Valdese Manufacturing Company in Valdese, was an inveterate raconteur. Concerned citizens had his name printed on the Valdese municipal ballot as a candidate for mayor without his consent. Their action angered Francis. He told a nonresident cotton broker who visited him a few days before the election that he would not qualify for the office if he was elected.

The broker returned to Valdese several weeks later and asked Francis what had happened in the election. Francis said, "The fools elected me." The broker inquired, "Did you qualify as mayor?" Francis replied, "I certainly did qualify. I have been sworn in and cussed out. If that doesn't qualify one for public office, I don't know what does."

❦ Lum Garrison, Morganton's longtime philosopher, was tall, slender, straight, and bald-headed. He wore a walrus mustache and presented a melancholy countenance when he was in a humorous mood. The witticisms he authored are past numbering. He had alternative ways to address those he encountered. He would say, "Hi there, millunaire," to those he deemed worth five dollars or more and "Hi there, sager," to those he believed had less wealth. He frequently used the contracted profanity "I dot" for emphasis.

Lum always kept a carefully folded ten-dollar bill in his watch pocket as a hedge against financial adversity.

Lum loved to kid people. He had borrowed fifty cents from an acquaintance in the old days when a dollar represented a day's wages. He decided to have some fun with his creditor, and delayed repaying the loan of the fifty cents. After a spell, the creditor began to put this question to Lum when he met him: "Mr. Garrison, how about paying me my fifty cents?"

Lum invariably removed the folded ten-dollar bill from his watch pocket, smoothed it out, and asked his creditor, "I dot, sager, have you got change for ten dollars?"

Change for ten dollars was scarce in Burke at that time, and the creditor was compelled to answer Lum in the negative. Lum would carefully refold the ten-dollar bill and restore it to his watch pocket.

The creditor became wearied of this experience, saved his surplus earnings until he had accumulated ten dollars in cash, and confronted Lum with a request for repayment of the fifty cents. Lum went through his customary procedure and asked his creditor, "I dot, sager, have you got change for ten dollars?"

"Yes, Mr. Garrison," his creditor promptly replied, "I've got it in my pocket."

Lum carefully folded up his ten-dollar bill, replaced it in his watch pocket, and affirmed, "I dot, millunaire, a fellow who's got change for ten dollars don't need no fifty cents."

❧   H. E. C. Bryant, a North Carolina native who was one of the famous reporters on the Washington scene at the time, visited John H. Pearson, a prominent resident of Morganton. Mr. Pearson suggested that Mr. Bryant, who was popularly known as "Red Buck Bryant" because of his flaming red hair, interview Lum on the issues of the day and write about the interview for the Sunday newspapers. Red Buck did so.

The interview occurred in the period preceding America's entry into the First World War. German submarines were sinking American merchant ships on the high seas. President Wilson had proposed that Congress arm American merchant ships and authorize them to fire on German submarines that attacked them.

This proposal had raised a hot issue, and Red Buck interviewed Lum on the subject. Lum told him he deemed the proposal very unwise because it was likely to get us into war with Germany. Red Buck interjected, "But, Mr. Garrison, there's such a thing as freedom of the seas, and our ships have the right to sail the high seas."

"That's right, Mr. Bryant," Lum said. "My friend Charlie McKesson lives on this end of Burkemont Avenue, and my friend John Pearson lives near the other end. If Mr. McKesson and Mr. Pearson fell out and began shooting at each other, I'd have the right to travel Burkemont Avenue, but I'd be a cussed fool if I did it."

🦌   Jock Fleming was a handsome fellow who had the strength of a giant. His only fault was that he sometimes drank a little too much corn liquor.

Jock and two of his friends were driving along the highway in a dilapidated Ford car. They were intoxicated. The car ran off the road. Fons Duckworth, Morganton's chief of police, was summoned. He found that Jock's friends were seriously injured and sent them to the hospital in an ambulance. Jock was so limber he suffered no injury. Chief Duckworth undertook to ascertain from Jock who was driving the Ford at the time of the accident so he could charge the driver with operating an automobile while under the influence of an intoxicating beverage.

To this end, Fons asked Jock, "Who was driving the Ford when it ran off the highway?"

" 'Fore God, Chief," Jock replied, " 'fore God, I don't know. The last thing I remember all of us were riding on the back seat."

🦌   Isaac T. Avery, of the Morganton bar, was one of Burke County's most engaging humorists. He laughed what he called Ma Brittain's fermentation case out of court in the most remarkable display of forensic humor I have ever observed. Mrs. Brittain was charged with illegally manufacturing wine. Mr. Avery's speech to the jury in her behalf had many hilarious twists and turns.

In essence, however, it presented to the jury this convincing argument: Ma Brittain was innocent of wrongdoing. She had done nothing except put some innocuous grape juice in some crocks. The real culprit was the Almighty, who had caused the innocuous grape juice to ferment in obedience to divine law.

❦   Of Mr. Avery's manifold anecdotes, my favorite is this:

John and Mary were sitting on a bench in the moonlight. The fragrance of flowers filled the air, and everything was conducive to romance. John asked Mary, "If you wasn't what you is, what would you like to be?" Mary replied, "An American Beauty Rose." She turned the question on him, "John, if you wasn't what you is, what would you like to be?" John responded, "An octopus." Mary asked, "What is an octopus?" John answered, "An animal or a fish or something that's got a thousand arms." Mary inquired, "If you were an octopus, what would you do with all those arms?" John replied, "I'd put every one of them around you." Mary said, "Stop your foolish talk. You ain't using the two arms you've got."

❦   As a practicing lawyer, I always advised clients to tell me the complete truth about matters in which they were involved. I warned them that if they failed to do so, I was likely to be taken by surprise when their cases were tried, and they were likely to sustain disastrous consequences.

I have thought in retrospect that one of my clients, Cars Mull, did not heed my advice and warning. Cars was violence-prone when intoxicated. According to a rumor, he and El Mitchell, who had been drinking together, were walking along the highway about midnight on Christmas Eve. Cars allegedly bludgeoned El and left him lying in an unconscious state in the highway.

Be these things as they may have been, El was found lying on the highway in a comatose condition with a serious wound on his head and was conveyed to the hospital by some Good Samaritan.

After El had been released from the hospital, his wife, Essie, swore out a warrant before our beloved justice of the peace, Uncle Billy Hallyburton, in which she averred that Cars Mull had committed a felonious assault and battery on her husband.

On the day of the preliminary hearing, I accompanied my client, Cars, who had assured me of his innocence, to Uncle Billy's court. Essie had accompanied El, the prosecution's only witness, to court.

After Uncle Billy had administered to him an oath to tell the truth, the whole truth, and nothing but the truth, El took the witness stand. Uncle Billy admonished El to tell what he knew about the charge that Cars had committed a felonious assault on him Christmas Eve.

El testified, "I don't know nothing about that."

Uncle Billy instructed El to tell him what had happened at the time named in the warrant.

"Mr. Hallyburton," El said, "I was walking along the road all by myself singing 'O, Little Town of Bethlehem,' and a limb fell off of an overhanging tree and struck me on the head."

Essie jumped to her feet and yelled, "El Mitchell, you liar, tell Mr. Hallyburton what you told me." El said, "Essie, I didn't tell you nothing." Uncle Billy dismissed the case for want of evidence.

Some days later Cars visited my office and asked me to draw up a document which caused me to suspect the truthfulness of the assurances of innocence he had given me, and that of the testimony El had given before Uncle Billy.

Cars asked me to draw what lawyers call a general release, specifying that for a consideration duly received by him, El Mitchell had released Cars Mull from liability for anything which may have happened at any time between the creation of the earth and the date of the release.

❧ Whether justly or not, Pink Mitchell, who lived in the Laurel community of Burke County and called everybody "Honey," had the reputation of retailing moonshine liquor. According to an ancient rumor, two ex-sheriffs of Burke County, Manly McDowell and Forrest Berry, visited Pink to replenish their supplies. At the time Pink's wife, who was one of the finest women I have ever known, was visibly enceinte. Manly offered to give Pink five dollars if his expected heir was a boy and he named him Forrest Berry, and Forrest Berry countered Manly's offer by promising to give Pink ten dollars in the event his expected heir was a boy and he named him Manly

McDowell. Mrs. Mitchell bore twin boys, who were named Manly McDowell Mitchell and Forrest Berry Mitchell, and Pink received the sums Manly McDowell and Forrest Berry had promised him.

Sometime later, Pink called at my office and said, "Honey, I'm going to need you at the big court." I said, "Tell me about your trouble." Pink said, "I found a bee tree down in the woods. I knew the Old Woman and Forry Berry and Manny McDowell would enjoy the honey. So I got my axe, returned to the woods, and started to cut down the bee tree. Somebody came up behind me, slapped me on the back, and said, 'Pink, you're under arrest.' I looked around and saw the deputy sheriff. 'What for?' I asked him. The deputy said, 'For being at that still.' I looked around again, and sure enough there was a still."

Ⓨ   Francis Garrou had been born in the Cottian Alps in Northern Italy, and was brought to Valdese, the Waldensian settlement in Burke County, when he was about sixteen years of age. After he grew to maturity, he became one of Burke County's most useful and beloved citizens. His sense of humor was incredible.

On becoming the Democratic nominee for Burke County's seat in the North Carolina House of Representatives in 1932, Francis toured the county with other Democrats who were seeking county offices. I heard him speak at Salem.

He said: "Fellow citizens, I'm in what General Sherman would call one hell of a fix. I'm all messed up in politics, and I don't know anything about politics. I haven't learned to lie like Sheriff Fred Ross and our other candidates have. To show what a poor politician I am, I don't even have a platform. My Republican opponent, Harry L. Milner, has advertised his platform in a full-page ad in the *Morganton News Herald*. It contains one or two sound planks and hundreds of rotten ones. In the sound planks, he tells us what he intends to do for us if he defeats me. I guess it will be all right for me to steal the sound planks he has put in his platform and put them into effect when I go down to Raleigh to represent you.

"By the way, you will recall that Mr. Milner represented our district in the State Senate in 1929, and may wonder, as I do, why he didn't do some of the good things he now promises us while he was in the Senate."

I digress to note that Mr. Milner, a native of upstate New York, had been a resident of Morganton for many years, and was held in the highest esteem by all the community. His father, who had been a gallant Union soldier during the Civil War, had moved from New York to Morganton in his twilight years and become a member of his son's family in a county in which countless descendants of Confederate soldiers had their habitations.

Francis continued: "My Republican friends say that you ought not to elect me to the legislature because my father and I were born in Italy across the sea. That's about the only thing truthful they're saying about me these days. I've lived in Burke County more years than my opponent and Homer Ballengee, the Republican candidate for sheriff, have lived in North Carolina and more years than Herbert Hoover, the Republican candidate for President, has lived in the United States. I can say one thing about my old father which my opponent can't say about his. My old father didn't put a gun on his shoulder and come marching down here from the North to kill any of your folks."

❦ Francis was overwhelmingly elected. While he was serving in the House, a newsman asked him, "How many terms have you served in the legislature?" Francis answered, "This is my first and my last."

The counties had been controlling the public schools and financing their operation with some aid from the state for periods of eight months each year. A bill came before the House providing for the state to assume control of all the public schools, to finance their operations in their entirety, and to extend their terms from eight to nine months. When the floor manager of the bill assured the House that the state could operate the schools for nine months more cheaply than the counties had been operating them for eight months, Francis arose and asked him if he did not think he ought to amend the bill. The floor manager said No, but stated he would be glad to consider any amendment Francis suggested. "I was thinking," Francis said, "that you might want to amend the bill by extending the school term to twelve months. That would enable the schools to declare dividends for the state's taxpayers at every commencement."

❧   A newsman saw Governor J. C. B. Ehringhaus, State Treasurer Charles Johnson, and Francis Garrou at the airport in Raleigh preparing to fly to New York.

The newsman asked Governor Ehringhaus why he and Charlie Johnson were going to New York. Governor Ehringhaus told him that North Carolina had been compelled to borrow millions of dollars to finance her services to the people since the Great Depression began in 1929 and that they were going to New York to try to persuade the Wall Street bankers to let North Carolina renew her notes.

When the newsman inquired of Francis as to why he was going to New York, Francis replied, "The governor and the treasurer are taking me along to have me endorse the notes if the bankers won't renew them without my becoming surety for the state."

❧   When he ministered to their hurts and ills, Dr. Edward W. Phifer, the elder of the name, dosed his patients with humor as healing as the medicines he prescribed.

One day long ago I was a passenger in the automobile of a friend which was involved in a collision with another motor vehicle. A piece of shattered and flying glass inflicted extensive cuts on my forehead and scalp. A Good Samaritan who happened by conveyed me to Dr. Phifer, who was at Grace Hospital in Morganton.

Although neither fact is germane to my story, I note that the collision occurred in the days of prohibition and that Dr. Phifer always deplored the use of alcohol for libation purposes.

On surveying my injury, Dr. Phifer advised me and the attending nurse, Grace Pearson, that my injury covered substantial space, that it would necessitate shaving a part of my scalp and require many stitches, and that pain-deadening injections were not adapted to alleviate the accompanying pain. He then asked Grace if there was any whiskey at hand. "Yes, some of the meanest moonshine ever brought to Grace Hospital," she replied. At his directions, Grace poured out a tumbler full of it, and I downed it.

Before the drink took its full effect, Dr. Phifer advised me that he was a better doctor than he was a barber and took a swipe at my scalp with a somewhat dull razor. I said, "Doctor, I *hope* you're a better physician than barber."

After Dr. Phifer had repaired, treated, and bandaged my wounds, Grace told me to go home and go to bed. "Don't you do anything of the kind," Dr. Phifer said. "It would be safer for you to put yourself once again in the middle of the highway. Bed is the most dangerous place on earth. Most people meet death there."

My good friend Ned Claywell, who was ever a help to me in trouble and who had driven to Grace Hospital on hearing of the accident, drove me home. On my arrival there, I discovered to my joy that my gentle mother-in-law had paid us a surprise visit. Emboldened by the mean moonshine, I remarked to her, "I'll have to explain to the community that it was entirely by unrelated coincidence I suffered my injury on the day my mother-in-law came to town."

❦ Dr. Phifer undertook to persuade Henry McKinney, the long-time janitor of Grace Hospital and its sponsor, Grace Episcopal Church, to quit drinking moonshine liquor, which was hard to come by and often of unknown ingredients during prohibition. To this end, Dr. Phifer gave him this warning: "One of these days you may drink something with wood alcohol in it. That would make you blind."

"Doctor, I'd sure hate for that to happen," Henry responded. "But I'm not going to give up drinking. I've seen about everything that's worth seeing."

❦ Henry was something of a humorist in his own right. During the days preceding absolute prohibition, North Carolina allowed each adult within her borders to receive by express one quart of bonded whiskey every fifteen days. At that time Grace Episcopal Church's rector was an English born and educated clergyman, the Reverend George Hilton, who shocked ardent drys by going to the express office every fifteen days, getting a quart of bottled in bond, stopping by a drugstore where soft drinks were available for use as chasers on his way to the rectory, and taking a drink in public en route home.

Henry overheard many drys express disapproval of this conduct of Mr. Hilton, who was succeeded in the rectorate of Grace Church by Norvin C. Duncan. After Henry had aided in installing the furniture of the Duncan family in the rectory, the sun was setting behind Table Rock and Hawks Bill Mountain in all its resplendent glory. As he watched the sunset, Mr. Duncan observed, "Henry, this is a beautiful town. I'd like to stay here a long time." Henry responded, "They'll let you if you'll only behave yourself."

❧   Caleb Kincaid, one of Burke County's most intriguing wits, made no discriminations in favor of his friends when he selected targets for his sarcastic shafts.

After the Great Depression made President Hoover the butt of jokers, Cale, an incorrigible Democrat, related this story.

He undertook to walk along the highway from Morganton to Rutherfordton carrying a placard reading, "Don't pick me up. I'm one of the fools who voted for Hoover." Within a couple of minutes a huge traffic jam ensued, and hundreds of motorists stopped their cars and begged him to ride with them.

Dr. Will Abernethy, who was one of Cale's boyhood contemporaries, became one of North Carolina's most distinguished, eloquent, and polished Methodist divines. After hearing him preach, Cale remarked, "I used to think a fellow had to have some religion to be a good preacher. Now I know better. I've heard Will Abernethy preach."

Cale's good friend, the late Herbert Walton, one of Morganton's prominent citizens, inherited his beautiful home, "Creekside," and many adjacent acres. Owing to the fertility of his acres of bottom land abutting on Silver Creek, Mr. Herbert was never compelled to labor with the diligence that was necessarily displayed by Burke County farmers who earned their livelihoods on farms lying on rocky ridges.

One day I was standing on the sidewalk adjacent to the Lazarus store talking to its owner, Harry L. Wilson, and Cale Kincaid. Herbert Walton came by and made this remark to Cale: "Cale, yesterday was my eightieth birthday anniversary, and I'm tired."

"I don't see how you can be tired, Herbert," Cale responded. "You've been resting for eighty years and one day."

ξ Cale and his friend Beauregard Mangum, who was called "Boney" by all who knew him, were unlike most Burke County men. They were not exceedingly handsome. They were at a picnic together near Bridgewater. At the suggestion of a wag, those attending the picnic cast paper ballots to determine the all-important question whether Cale or Boney was the ugliest man present.

When the ballots were counted, it appeared that a majority of them had accorded the dubious distinction to Cale. He forthwith demanded a rerun, alleging that there had been rascality in the voting or the tabulation of the votes.

ξ My wife and I were married at the old First Presbyterian Church in her home town of Concord on June 18, 1924. I was the Democratic candidate for Burke County's seat in the North Carolina House of Representatives in the ensuing election in November.

North Carolina did not enjoy secret balloting at that time. State, district, county, and local ballots, and the ballots of the political parties were paper ballots printed separately. Any voter could indulge in split voting by striking out the name of the candidate on the ballot of one party and writing in its place the name of the opposing candidate of another party.

Any voter could secure ballots of the party of his registration from the precinct election officials and obtain assistance in marking them from any person he chose before casting them. Electioneering near polls was allowed.

Mrs. Ned Claywell, an ardent Democrat, had arranged for various Democratic women, including my wife, to set up card tables near four polling places at the old historic Burke County Courthouse to aid Democrats in marking their ballots.

On ascertaining my wife's identity, Cale Kincaid went to her table and pretended he had no idea who she was. He told her that he was a

Democrat who split his voting in rare instances when he deemed Democratic candidates to be rascals; that he could not read or write; and that he needed her assistance in marking his ballots, which he presented to her.

As a newcomer to Morganton, my wife did not know Caleb. When she expressed to him in her gracious way the hope that he did not wish to indulge in split voting on that occasion, Cale remarked, "I certainly do. There are two damned rascals on the Democratic ticket. One of them is Furnifold M. Simmons, who is running for the United States Senate, and the other is Sam Ervin, who is running for the legislature."

With rare exceptions, small-town barbers are very talkative. Ted Shirley, my barber and friend, followed his vocation for many years as one of the five barbers in Collett Parks's shop in Morganton. Ted was noted for his sense of humor and for regaling his patrons at great length with his views on all subjects.

One day I entered Parks's shop, saw Ted standing at the mirror shaving himself, observed his four co-workers seated in idleness, and inquired, "Ted, why don't you get a good barber to do your barber-work for you?" Ted paused, looked hard at his co-workers, and responded, "I would, but I'd hate to go out of town just to get a shave."

Harry Hallyburton, a public school principal, is a devotee of local history. He spends much time in old cemeteries reading and recording the epitaphs on gravestones. I was seated in another barber's chair getting a hair-cut, and Harry was seated in Ted's chair for the like purpose. Ted asked Harry, "Why are you always wandering around in old cemeteries and reading the epitaphs on the gravestones?" Harry forthwith responded, "I'm looking for a silent barber."

Chapter 3

Humor in Education

ɞ ɞ ɞ

Years before the Supreme Court of the United States handed down its decisions in the school prayer cases, students in the Morganton High School were required to answer the morning roll call with quotations from the Scriptures.

I answered the roll call one morning with this quotation: "I have more understanding than all my teachers." The quotation moved my classmates to laughter and my teacher to anger. She punished me by keeping me after school and requiring me to memorize and recite Thomas Gray's "Elegy Written in a Country Churchyard."

When I protested it was unfair to punish me because I had quoted the Bible correctly as I was supposed to do, my teacher said that the words I quoted were not in the Bible. After I called her attention to Psalms 119, verses 99–100, she conceded that I had quoted the Bible correctly, but asserted that I nevertheless deserved the punishment imposed on me because I did not quote it with reverence.

ɞ Burke County's two most productive educators of all time were Logan Patton and his son, Robert L. Patton, who was known as Rob Patton. Logan Patton spent his boyhood on his father's farm near Table Rock during the early days of Reconstruction, when the defeated South lay prostrate and poverty stricken. It undoubtedly seemed to him at times that his desire to acquire a collegiate education and become a teacher of youth was nothing more than a haunting dream. He nevertheless clung to it with indomitable tenacity.

One night young Logan's father sent him to the woodpile for some wood to replenish the fire in an open fireplace. En route to the woodpile, he decided to begin his quest for an education without delay.

Instead of complying with his father's instruction, he left home with fifteen cents in his pocket and traveled, mostly on foot, to Illinois, paying his expenses at all times by hard labor. He stayed in Illinois for a while attending preparatory schools in various places. He then went to New England, where he worked his way through Phillips Academy in Vermont and Amherst College in Massachusetts. After graduating at Amherst in 1876, he returned to Burke County to inaugurate his teaching career. En route to his old home, he stopped at the woodpile, picked up an armful of firewood, and walked into his father's presence with the statement, "Father, here's the firewood you sent me after eleven years ago."

❧   Logan Patton's first school was a one-room schoolhouse in Jonas Ridge Township, Burke County's most mountainous subdivision. He boarded with a mountain family and shared a bedroom with the grandfather of the family, whose long beard fell below his waist.

On their first evening together, Logan and the old mountaineer conversed with each other before a fire in an open fireplace. After they had exhausted other subjects of conversation, Logan asked the old mountaineer, "What do you do with your beard when you retire for the night? Do you put it under the cover, or do you leave it outside the cover?"

The old mountaineer replied, "I've had my beard for fifty years, but I've never thought about what I do with it when I go to bed. I can't tell you that."

After several hours of refreshing sleep, Logan was aroused by a noise. Observing the old man pacing to and fro between the beds and the dying embers in the open fireplace, he told him that he hoped he was not ill. "No, I'm not sick," the mountaineer responded. "It's that question you asked that's troubling me. When I got in bed, I wondered what I did do with my beard at night. I put it under the cover. That didn't seem natural, and I couldn't sleep. I put it outside the cover. That didn't seem right, and I couldn't sleep. I wish you hadn't asked me that question."

❧   On attaining adulthood, Rob Patton followed in his father's footsteps. After serving as a classroom teacher, he became Burke County's superintendent of schools, and filled that post with distinction for thirty-nine years. As a speaker, Rob was noted for his humor and his capacity to coin aphorisms. Of many terse sayings attributed to him, my favorite is this: "Life is a grindstone. Whether it grinds you down or polishes you up depends on you."

When I enrolled as a freshman at the University of North Carolina in September, 1913, I was assigned to an 8:30 A.M. class in American history, which met in a lecture room on the second floor of the Old West Building and was taught by Professor Daniel Huger Bacot, a descendant of the French Huguenots of Charleston, South Carolina. Professor Bacot had a dour countenance, and no one suspected he possessed a sense of humor.

On Halloween some mischievous students, who were bent on embarrassing the supposedly humorless professor, managed to lead a cow up the steps to the lecture room and tie her to the corner of Professor Bacot's desk.

News of this spread abroad, and all of the members of the class were in their seats before the time scheduled for its opening the following morning. Professor Bacot entered the classroom and cast a fleeting glance at the cow, which stood beside his desk quietly chewing her cud. After so doing, the professor said, "Young gentlemen, I'm delighted to observe that the intellectual strength of my audience has increased so much since my last lecture." He then lectured on American history for an hour without paying any more heed to the cow.

Dr. Vernon Howell, dean of the School of Pharmacy at Chapel Hill, was an enduring hero on the campus. Each generation of students in those days who witnessed the recurring defeats Carolina's football team suffered remembered him as the player who made a winning touchdown against Carolina's arch rival, the University of Virginia, about 1905.

Dr. Howell kept bachelor quarters in Chapel Hill. He had an arbor behind his house which was famed for its luscious grapes. At that time all the mail coming to faculty, students, and townspeople reached the Chapel Hill post office about noon, and they gathered there to see what the day had brought them.

One of my closest friends at Chapel Hill was Clinton Kelly

Hughes, of Asheville, who subsequently became an able member of the Buncombe County bar. My story requires me to reveal a peccadillo of Clinton's. I cannot obtain his prior consent to make the revelation because the Good Lord called him to heaven years ago. Knowing him as I did, however, I am confident he would not object to my story either here or in the hereafter.

Clinton and I were attending summer school at Chapel Hill. He had to repeat and pass a course which was prerequisite to obtaining the degree he sought. We met in front of the post office. I asked Clinton how the final examination in his course, which he had taken that morning, had gone.

He replied, "Fine. It was easy. I'm sure I passed. I'm afraid, however, I'll be shipped for stealing Dr. Howell's grapes before I can get my degree."

He had gone to Dr. Howell's arbor to purloin grapes the previous evening. Dr. Howell had opened his back door and called out, "Who's stealing my grapes?" and he had fled. On reaching his dormitory room, he discovered he had lost some letters addressed to him and was sure he had dropped them under the grape arbor in his haste. They would be found, and he would be expelled for stealing grapes.

At that juncture I saw Dr. Howell making a beeline for us. When he reached us, Dr. Howell asked Clinton, "Are you Clinton K. Hughes?" On receiving an affirmative answer, Dr. Howell said, "Mr. Hughes, a thief undertook to steal some of my grapes last evening. When I called out, he fled. I discovered that the same thief had previously stolen some letters addressed to you. After he fled, I found them under my grape arbor, and I am pleased to return them to you." With that, Dr. Howell handed Clinton his letters, turned abruptly, and began to walk away.

Clinton had been too flabbergasted to thank Dr. Howell, who suddenly spun around and called to Clinton, "By the way, Mr. Hughes, if you like grapes, come down to my arbor, bring some of your friends with you, and enjoy my grapes. I've never raised any finer."

That was only one of the many instances in which Dr. Howell revealed himself as a man with an understanding heart.

❦   When I was a justice of the North Carolina Supreme Court, my wife and I lived in Raleigh, and our daughter Leslie, who was a first-year student at Duke University, often visited us on weekends. Leslie always made superlative grades as a student.

On one of her weekend visits, Leslie was totally incapacitated by illness. When she was advised to take to bed, she declared she could not, because she had to write a theme for delivery to her teacher in creative writing on the following Monday.

I asked Leslie what the subject of her theme was required to be. She replied that the theme had to discuss the procedure or system by which an organization performed its tasks.

"Go to bed," I said. "Your problem is solved. While I know that it would not be according to Hoyle, I will write a theme for you on how the Supreme Court of North Carolina performs its judicial tasks, and you can turn it in. I'm sure the Recording Angel will note your illness, and drop a tear which will wash out any iniquity of your doing that."

Leslie went to bed. I wrote what I deemed an excellent article on the procedure by which the North Carolina Supreme Court performed its judicial tasks, typewrote it carefully, and gave it to Leslie as she was returning to Duke.

Leslie has always been most conscientious. Consequently, I have never been fully satisfied that she delivered the theme I wrote to her teacher. In any event, Leslie told me on her next visit that she had delivered the theme to her teacher and that her teacher had graded it "4 minus" and returned it to her with this notation: "This is far inferior to your usual performance."

❦   As a youth, I envied the satisfaction that tobacco-chewers derived from indulging in their habit. They resembled contented cows chewing their cuds. During my student days at Chapel Hill chewing tobacco was the most prevalent of the discountenanced habits of students.

I soon succumbed to it. Under the tutorage of Coleman Hall, of Webster, North Carolina, I acquired proficiency in accurate expectoration. As a consequence, I entered the Tobacco Chewers Tournament, which was then held annually in front of Old South Building, and won the highest award, a Brown Mule tobacco tag suspended on a long blue ribbon, for accuracy in long-distance expectoration.

Years afterward my beloved classmate Ernest Lloyd Mackie asserted at a public meeting in Chapel Hill that during my student days I sometimes indulged in the lowest form of wit—punning. To bolster his accusation, he added that during a debate in the Dialectic Literary Society he heard me make this statement to characterize my opponent's speech: "When an oration we expect, we get expectoration."

When I graduated at Chapel Hill in 1917, the *Yackety Yack*, the annual student publication, contained a cartoon depicting me with my right cheek vastly extended by a hidden chew of Picnic Twist Tobacco and engaging in a good-bye handshake with a being labeled "Mr. Chawing Weed," who was warning me I'd miss him after leaving Chapel Hill.

I have been missing "Mr. Chawing Weed" ever since I married. My wife exercised her authoritative power and compelled me to give up chewing tobacco.

My good friend Thomas J. Harkins, of Asheville, one-time United States district attorney for the Western District of North Carolina and afterward sovereign grand commander of the Ancient and Accepted Scottish Rite Masons of the Southern Jurisdiction of the United States, preserved his right to chew tobacco much later in life.

Tom purchased an ornate cuspidor and installed it in his study at home. After dinner each evening, he would repair to his study and chew tobacco and read. One evening he discovered that his cuspidor was missing. He called his charming helpmate, Miss Roxanna, and told her, "Dear, I'm missing my cuspidor." Miss Roxanna smiled and responded, "Yes, Tom. You've been missing it. That's why I gave it away today."

❦   I had heard a story, which was attributed to Dr. Charles W. Elliott, a distinguished president of Harvard University. When someone asked him why Harvard had the reputation of being a great depository of learning, Dr. Elliott is reputed to have replied: "The only explanation I can give is that freshmen bring so much learning to Harvard, and the seniors take such a little bit away."

I do not know whether this story influenced my decision, but I decided to attend Harvard Law School after I had passed the bar examination and been licensed to practice law in North Carolina in August, 1919.

At that time I was deeply in love with the girl who is now my wife, as I have always been since I first saw her, and was competing for her affections with many rivals. I believed that the adage that "absence makes the heart grow fonder" applied to those near at hand rather than those far away.

Consequently, I decided to attend Harvard Law School for one year only, and enrolled as a special student in the third-year class. After that year the object of my affections agreed that she would not enter into any entangling alliance with any of my rivals while I was attending Harvard Law School a second year, and I enrolled in the second-year class. As that year was expiring, we reached a more enduring understanding, and I descended to the first-year class and obtained a Bachelor of Laws degree from Harvard Law School, which was printed in Latin and which my educational deficiency disabled me to read.

I believe I am the only person who ever went through Harvard Law School backward.

꙾ My most joyous moments at Harvard were spent at a table in the dining room in Memorial Hall, which had been erected and so designated to honor the Harvard men who had made the supreme sacrifice fighting for the Union and against the Confederacy.

A congenial group of law students gathered at this table three times daily and exchanged views and banter. In addition to me, the group included Thurman Castello and Floyd Crouse, who had been college mates of mine at Chapel Hill; George Smucker of Dallas, Texas; and young men from the states of California, Massachusetts, Mississippi, Nebraska, Ohio, Tennessee, and Washington.

George Smucker loved to poke fun at everybody and everything. Our tablemate from Massachusetts brought a guest to lunch one day. He explained that Memorial Hall was a memorial to the Harvard men who had died in the Civil War. "You're wrong," George said, "It's a monument to the accuracy of Southern marksmanship."

One Sunday some of us attended services with George in the

magnificent First Church of Christ, Scientist, in Boston. When we assembled for our evening repast, George asked us what was the most impressive thing about the service. One said one thing, and others said other things. George said, "You're all wrong. The most impressive thing was that the whole congregation had bad colds."

🦗   Floyd Crouse had a quiet, but somewhat devastating, sense of humor. Our California tablemate, Connolly, was one of those chronically loyal sons of California who seized every opportunity to boast of the infinite superiority of everything Californian over everything else in the universe.

The morning newspapers carried an item recounting the discovery of the skull of a prehistoric man near Santa Barbara, California, and disclosing the speculation of some anthropologists that the discovery indicated that California had the first climate in America where human life could exist.

When he came to breakfast, Connolly bubbled over with enthusiasm, and invoked the newspaper item as a basis for the unlimited extolling of California's climate. Floyd said, "Connolly, I'm surprised you had not heard about the discovery of this skull before this. I read about it in a scientific journal some weeks ago. The journal not only related everything about the discovery of the skull but it revealed the identity of the person whose skull it had been, and the circumstances surrounding his death."

Connolly interrupted Floyd, "That's wonderful. What did the scientific journal say?"

Floyd continued, "The journal said the skull was that of the original Californian, that he had been slain by an irate tourist while bragging on the California climate, that the court had granted the tourist's motion for a change of venue to Nevada, and that the Nevada court had acquitted the tourist because it concluded the slaying was justifiable homicide."

🦗   As long as time lasts for me, I will treasure in my memory sitting at the feet of Dean Roscoe Pound, Samuel Williston, Joseph Beale, Edward Warren, Austin Wakefield Scott, Joseph Warren, Zachariah Chafee, and Calvert Magruder in Harvard Law School.

Dean Pound had a most remarkable memory. He could lecture for an hour without notes explaining the niceties of the law and citing by volume cases from all Anglo-American jurisdiction in support of what he said. He gave this exhortation to his students: "You must know the law like a sailor knows his ship, drunk or sober."

Sometimes Dean Pound would relax and tell this story. As a young lawyer, he practiced with an established law firm in Omaha, Nebraska, which represented all the railroads serving the area. He was sent to a rural community to try a petty case for a railroad before an old justice of the peace, who happened to be a good friend of the senior member of the firm. As plaintiff, the railroad sought to recover demurrage from a merchant on a shipment of freight.

The justice of the peace ruled in favor of the plaintiff. Dean Pound said that it was unusual for a railroad to win a law suit in those days and that he bragged of his victory before the justice of the peace on his return to the offices of the firm in Omaha.

His opportunity for boasting proved short-lived. After a few days, the old justice visited the senior member of the firm and told him, "You sent a young whipper-snapper to try a case before me a few days ago. He tried to make me believe that the railroad was the plaintiff. He couldn't fool me. I knew the railroad could not be a plaintiff, and so I gave judgment for the plaintiff as usual."

❦   Edward Warren, who was known as "Bull" Warren, was a terror. Although he afterward explained his teaching methods in his little book *Spartan Education* in erudite language, I believe I may be able to explain them in more realistic fashion.

On the opening day each year, Bull Warren would say to his students, "Look at the students on your right and left. One of the three of you won't be back next year because of poor grades."

Each teacher in the Harvard Law School had charts that revealed the names of his students and their respective seats in his classrooms. During my days at Harvard, most of the law students were veterans of the First World War who had endured the perils of battle. When Bull Warren questioned his students, he took up the chart and proceeded to question the students in the exact sequence in which their names appeared in one of its rows. Consequently, each

student could anticipate when he was about to be subjected to interrogation. Sometimes students who had faced German machine guns
without faltering descended to the floor and crawled under the seats
to the door and made their exits from the classroom rather than
endure the sarcasm that they anticipated Warren would visit on
them if they gave an erroneous answer to a question.

Samples may illustrate why his students dreaded the prospect of
being targets of his sarcasm. One day a student made a poor response to one of his questions, and Warren commented, "Some students will never become lawyers. They ought to choose another
vocation. I suggest that you study music or write poetry."

On another occasion he told a student he was going to interrogate
him on law and that he hoped the student would make a noise like a
lawyer in answering. He then proceeded to state three times in rapid
succession the facts in cases, reveal the rulings the courts handed
down in such cases, and ask the student whether he deemed the
rulings to be legally sound. The student gave this succinct reply to
each question, "I can conceive of the court making its ruling on the
facts." Warren exploded, "You've conceived three times and haven't
given birth to a single thought."

Bull Warren was a profound legal scholar. He had no patience
with mediocrity in the classroom. As he afterward confessed, he was
a Spartan teacher. Whether the irascibility he exhibited in the
classroom was actual or feigned I do not know. But I do know he was
the gentlest of souls outside the classroom.

❧ Felix Frankfurter had already attained his merited reputation
as one of America's finest scholars. I have always regretted that I
did not sit at his feet during my days at Harvard Law School. I was
deterred from taking his course on public utilities by this warning:
"If you want to know what Frankfurter thinks about everything
in the universe except public utilities, take his course on public
utilities."

After Frankfurter became a Supreme Court justice and I became a
United States senator, I fought a civil rights proposal on the ground,
among others, that it denied the right of trial by jury in civil contempt proceedings. One evening at twilight I was standing on the
sidewalk abutting on Constitution Avenue trying to get a taxicab to

take me to the National Press Club Building. One taxicab after another rushed by with passengers and without stopping. A private automobile stopped at the curb, and one of its occupants, whom I could not identify in the deepening twilight, asked, "Senator, can't I give you a ride?" I thanked the speaker, and declined his invitation because I did not want to take him out of his way.

The taxicabs continued to rush by with passengers and without stopping. The speaker in the automobile said, "You're having trouble getting a cab. Maybe you won't take me out of my way." When I told him I was going to the National Press Club, he said, "I have to pass within half a block of it on my way home," and opened the door to admit me into the automobile.

I then recognized that the speaker was Justice Frankfurter, who was being driven home by a law clerk. As I entered the automobile, the justice stuck out his hand and said, "Frankfurter's my name." I said, "Yes, Judge. I deeply appreciate your courtesy to me."

When the automobile resumed its movement, Justice Frankfurter remarked, "I'm informed you're taking the arguments of the liberals, and using them to defeat a civil rights bill." "I'm trying to," I observed. "And the most potent arguments I've found are in an article by James M. Landis and a fellow named Felix Frankfurter, which appeared in the *Harvard Law Review* in 1923."

Justice Frankfurter laughed and said, "They called me a liberal in those days. Nowadays they call me everything that's opprobrious."

᷀ During my days at Harvard Law School, I belonged to the Southern Club of Harvard, which sponsored delightful dances at frequent intervals at the Copley-Plaza Hotel in Boston.

Floyd Crouse, my longtime friend and schoolmate, was squiring a beautiful Wellesley College student to these dances and other social events. She advised him she would like for Floyd to get one of his friends to invite her roommate to be his dancing partner at the forthcoming Southern Club dance. Floyd drafted me for this assignment. Neither Floyd nor I had ever met his girl's roommate.

We met Floyd's girl and her roommate at the Copley-Plaza Hotel on the evening of the dance. We were somewhat surprised by the roommate's appearance because she was enormously fat.

Although she had much charm as well as much avoirdupois, the members of the Southern Club of Harvard laid aside their customary chivalry and did not dance with my dancing partner at any time. As a consequence, I spent what seemed to me to be an eternity piloting her on the ballroom floor. It is hardly an exaggeration to say that every time she took a step, the Copley-Plaza trembled.

Finally, Floyd realized he was in some degree responsible for my plight. During a short intermission, he whispered to me, "I will dance the next dance with your partner." I whispered my thanks to him and stated, "I want to go to the lobby and smoke." Floyd entreated me in a whisper, "Don't smoke but once." I gave him my whispered promise that I would obey his entreaty.

I went to the lobby and purchased for fifty cents the biggest and longest cigar the operator of the vending counter had. I digress to observe that these events occurred in the preinflationary era when one could buy a big and long cigar for fifty cents.

I seated myself in a luxurious chair in the lobby, lighted my cigar, and smoked it until its ignited end threatened to burn my lips. I then threw the stub of the cigar into a cuspidor, returned to the ballroom with a dispatch no greater than what has been described since as deliberate speed, and assumed a position at the edge of the ballroom floor.

After Floyd had piloted my dancing partner to my vicinity several times, I relieved him and resumed my dancing with her. As I did so, Floyd whispered, "You didn't keep your promise." I returned the whispered reply, "I kept my promise faithfully. I only smoked one big and long fifty-cent cigar."

❦   During the six years before I took my first oath as a senator, I was a justice of the North Carolina Supreme Court. Much to the dismay of many judges and lawyers, the Supreme Court of the United States was then accelerating its judicial activism. I digress to observe that a judicial activist is a judge who interprets the Constitution to mean what it would have said if he instead of the Founding Fathers had written it.

While serving on the North Carolina Supreme Court I was an orthodox judge. I refrained from discussing publicly the judicial activism of United States Supreme Court justices as well as all political issues.

Shortly after I became a senator and gained freedom from judicial orthodoxy, I accepted an invitation to speak to the Harvard Law School Association of New York City. In preparing my remarks, I reread Federalist Papers Nos. 78 and 81, in which Alexander Hamilton took note of the arguments of Elbridge Gerry and George Mason, who opposed ratification of the Constitution on the ground that it lacked provisions making it mandatory for Supreme Court justices to adhere to their oaths to support it and thus left them free to substitute their personal notions for constitutional precepts while professing to interpret them.

Hamilton asserted that Supreme Court justices would be faithful to their oaths and declared that "the supposed danger of judiciary encroachments . . . is, in reality, a phantom." I prepared remarks somewhat critical of recent Supreme Court decisions and entitled them "Alexander Hamilton's Phantom."

Dean Erwin Griswold introduced me to the Law School Association at an evening banquet in New York. At the outset, I said, "I want to absolve my legal alma mater, Harvard Law School, and my host, the Law School Association, from complicity in the crime I'm going to commit. They cannot be accessories before the fact because they don't know what I am about to do. They cannot be aiders or abettors because they are not going to encourage my crime while I'm committing it. They cannot be accessories after the fact because they will not offer me any haven after the crime is committed.

"Harvard Law School cannot be convicted of complicity on the theory of guilt by association because it's been a long time since it's had any association with me. But if the Law School feels the need of positive evidence of its innocence, I can furnish it the name of a friend who recently introduced me to an audience in North Carolina with these words: 'I understand our speaker is a graduate of the Harvard Law School, but, thank God, no one would ever suspect it.' I don't know whether he was speaking in defense of Harvard Law School or in defense of me."

When I completed my remarks and sat down, I observed to my right-hand dinner companion, United States Circuit Judge Learned Hand, whom I had met for the first time that evening, that I hated to be so critical of our highest judicial tribunal. Judge Hand said, "You ought not to be. You told the truth."

I did not know until he spoke that Judge Hand was among the many excellent judges who deplored the judicial activism of Supreme Court justices. He afterward disclosed his views on this subject publicly when he delivered the Oliver Wendell Holmes Lectures at Harvard.

❧ Judge Learned Hand was one of America's most knowledgeable and impartial jurists. If some president had had the good judgment to name him to the Supreme Court, he would have stood out in history as one of the greatest Supreme Court justices of all time.

In my rare moments of pessimism, I am constrained to believe that the American people were denied the blessing of Judge Hand's service on the Supreme Court either because politically powerful pressure groups who sometimes influence appointments to the court realized he would not give priority to their selfish demands in his rulings or because he never happened to be the crony of any president.

❧ Oscar Sikes, who subsequently became an outstanding attorney in Monroe, North Carolina, loved to live the good life while he was a student at Wake Forest University. As a consequence, he was somewhat ill-prepared when the time for examinations came. He was morally certain he had flunked all of them. As he was walking across the campus in a despondent mood, he encountered a religious fanatic, who asked him where he expected to spend eternity. He responded without hesitation, "If I wait until I get my bachelor's degree, I'll spend it at Wake Forest."

❧ The Norfolk and Western Railroad Company used to operate a passenger train, at the behest of the Women's Club of West Jefferson, North Carolina, as an excursion on its railroad between West Jefferson and Abingdon, Virginia, once a year after nature had tinted the autumn leaves with crimson and gold. The train, which was the only passenger train to move on the line, was known as the "Virginia Creeper," and was patronized by hundreds of joyous passengers.

My wife and I had the pleasure of traveling on the Virginia Creeper several times. On one occasion, I had the good fortune to be seated beside Richard Chase, a professional writer, who was then living in Beech Mountain School District in the nearby mountainous county of Avery. Mr. Chase told me two intriguing stories, one about Granny Mag and the other about Mr. Blank, teacher of science in the Beech Mountain High School. The Granny Mag story has no relevancy to education. I tell it at this point, however, because it is a good story, and this disposition of it will avoid some repetition elsewhere.

On the return trip from Abingdon, Granny Mag, an aged mountain matriarch, became troubled by the thought that the slow speed of the train might prevent her return home in time for her to perform her chores before dark. Every time the conductor passed through the car in which she was riding, Granny asked him, "Captain, can't you get the engineer to speed up the train? I'm afraid I won't get home in time to perform my chores before dark." The conductor politely explained to Granny Mag time after time that the engine was pulling many overloaded cars; that the route was mostly downhill; that if the engineer increased the speed of the train, he might have to apply the brakes suddenly to meet an unexpected emergency; and that in that event some cars might be derailed and some passengers seriously injured.

After a time Granny Mag's oft-repeated question irritated the conductor. "Granny Mag," he sarcastically remarked, "I'll ask the engineer to stop the train and let you alight and walk on ahead if you want me to." Granny Mag said, "Thank you, Captain, thank you. I'll not ask you to do that. They're not expecting me nohow till the train gits in."

❧ Richard Chase told me that he had met one of the committeemen of Beech Mountain School District a few days before and the committeeman had said, "Mr. Chase, I reckon you've heard that the school board met a few evenings ago and decided not to renew Mr. Blank's contract for next year." Mr. Chase told the committeeman, "That's news to me. I'm sorry to hear it. I understand Mr. Blank is one of the highest-educated men in the North Carolina public school system—that he has earned graduate degrees at many universities."

The committeeman responded, "That's so, Mr. Chase. That's the reason we're letting Mr. Blank go. He's been educated way past his intelligence."

❧ The Alumni Association of the University of North Carolina at Chapel Hill chose me as its president in 1947. When Joseph Maryon ("Spike") Saunders, its permanent executive secretary, and I were making plans for the next alumni luncheon, which was always held on the Monday during the university's commencement, we knew we had a problem which recent Alumni Association officials had been unable to solve.

Although they were seldom on the regular luncheon program, four of the university's most distinguished graduates, Josephus Daniels, publisher of the Raleigh *News and Observer*, John J. Parker, chief judge of the United States Court of Appeals for the Fourth Circuit, William Rand Kenan, donor of the beautiful Kenan Stadium, and John Motley Morehead, donor of the Morehead Planetarium and founder of the Morehead Scholarships, were always in attendance. Their many admirers among luncheon guests invariably called on them for remarks, and they invariably answered their calls. As a result, the alumni luncheon, which began at 12:30 P.M., continued for four hours or more, to the dismay of alumni officials and many others in attendance.

Spike said, "I wish there was some way for the alumni luncheon to adjourn at a more reasonable hour." I said, "Spike, it's going to do that next time." "I don't believe it," Spike said. "The age of miracles is past."

After the regular luncheon program had been completed at the next alumni luncheon, I did not give the admirers of any of our most distinguished alumni any opportunity to call on any of them for remarks. I stated, "I'm happy to observe that Josephus Daniels, John Parker, William Rand Kenan, and John Motley Morehead are among us. I ask them to stand at this time and take a bow."

They arose together to mighty applause. Without waiting for the applause to subside, I struck the podium a resounding blow with the gavel and declared, "The luncheon is adjourned."

Spike heaved a sigh of relief, smiled, and said, "The age of miracles has returned."

꿏   While I was serving on the North Carolina Supreme Court, my daughter Leslie was a student at Chapel Hill. Her favorite teacher was Hugh T. Lefler, Kenan Professor of History and author of monumental works on North Carolina's history. One weekend Leslie visited her mother and me in Raleigh and predicted that the university would tender me an honorary doctorate at its forthcoming commencement.

She based her prediction on this circumstance. Dr. Lefler, a member of the faculty committee on honorary degrees, had entered the classroom the day before, stared at her intently, and said, "The time for commencement is approaching when universities confer honorary degrees on some because of their merit and on others because of the public offices they occupy."

Leslie's prediction proved true. The university bestowed on me its honorary LL.D. degree in 1952.

꿏   During my Senate years I had the privilege of visiting Yale University twice, once to receive the Yale Student Union's A. Whitney Griswold Award, and once to serve as Chubb Visiting Fellow.

On the first occasion I had the pleasure of being an overnight guest in the home of President and Mrs. Kingman Brewster. After the meeting, Dr. Brewster observed, "The members of the Student Union are sometimes rough on speakers. They treated you gently. The only time they booed you was when your introducer said that you had attended Harvard Law School."

Harvard and Yale have been numbered for generations among the outstanding institutions of higher learning in the nation and the world. The champions of each of them sometimes indulge in humorous comments concerning the other. This practice has even produced some doggerel verse, which I quote from memory, and which treats Yale kindlier than Harvard.

> Here's to the crimson of Harvard,
> The land of the bean and the cod;
> Where the Cabots and Dodges
> Talk only to Lodges,
> And Lodges talk only to God.

> Here's to dear old New Haven,
> The Land of humility and light;
> Where God speaks to Jones
> In exactly the same tones
> He uses to Timothy Dwight.

My three days as Chubb Visiting Fellow were happy and busy ones. I spoke to twenty different groups, including a class in the Yale Divinity School.

❦   Shortly after my retirement from the Senate, I accepted an invitation from Chancellor Ferebee Taylor temporarily to join the faculty of my alma mater, the University of North Carolina at Chapel Hill, as a visiting Kenan Professor and to deliver lectures to law and political science students. While I enjoyed doing so very much, I experienced relief when my task ended because I realized that I had told the students everything I knew and would have been compelled to do some hard studying if I had tarried any longer.

❦   When my daughter Laura Powe was a wee tot, I asked her if she wanted half of an apple. She replied, "Yes, Daddy. Give me the biggest half."

As a former teacher of English in Concord High School, my wife sought to teach our children to speak correctly. She had difficulty persuading Laura Powe to stop saying "ain't." She repeatedly told her the expression did not constitute good speech, because there is no such word in the English language. Laura Powe finally confessed she had absorbed the instruction. She said, "Mother, I know ain't ain't a good word because there ain't no ain't."

Despite early deficiencies in math and grammar, Laura Powe had an exceedingly alert mind and was an excellent student. But she never aspired to recognition as a scholar. After her brother, Sam, made Phi Beta Kappa at Davidson and her sister Leslie achieved the like distinction at the University of North Carolina at Chapel Hill, Laura Powe warned me, "We've run out of Phi Betas in this family." "That's fine," I assured her. "I want one of you to be dumb like your dad."

Chapter 4

Humor in the Military

ও ও ও

Fitzhugh Lee, a nephew of the immortal Robert E. Lee, served with valor as major general of the cavalry of the Confederacy in the fratricidal war the North calls the "Civil War" and the South, the "War between the States." After that tragic confrontation, Fitzhugh Lee endeavored to unify the nation and served as the governor of his beloved Virginia.

In campaigning for the governorship, he exemplified an understanding of the political truth that a candidate may win the approval of his constituency by self-belittling humor. The following story was a fixture in his campaign speeches.

"After General Robert E. Lee had surrendered to General Ulysses S. Grant at Appomattox, I mounted my horse, and began my journey home. After I had proceeded down the road for several miles, I met a group of Confederate soldiers led by a sergeant and corporal, who were double-timing toward Appomattox. I halted them and inquired of the sergeant, 'Why are you all running to Appomattox?' The sergeant replied, 'We're going to join General Lee for the battle.' I said, 'Sergeant, it's no use. General Lee has surrendered.' The sergeant cast a doubting glance at me, and said to the corporal, 'Fitzhugh Lee may have surrendered, but not Marse Robert.'"

ও During the 1890s the people of Newton, the county seat of Catawba County, North Carolina, set aside a day in August of each year which they designated as Old Soldiers' Day, to pay tribute to Confederate veterans. After all the Confederate veterans had pitched their tents on fame's eternal camping ground, the people of Newton continued to celebrate Old Soldiers' Day, and to this day use it as an occasion for honoring all the soldiers who have served in all of America's wars.

Charles F. McKesson, a beloved member of the Morganton bar during my youth, was affectionately called "Cousin Charlie" by all the people of the community. He was a silver-tongued orator, in the parlance of the day, and was in great demand as a public speaker on occasions of patriotic rejoicing.

I told Cousin Charlie that he always spoke with grace and ease, and that I sometimes wondered whether he had ever lost his composure while speaking.

He responded, "Yes," and added, "I lost it completely years ago when I was keynote speaker at the Old Soldiers' Day in Newton.

"At that time multitudes of Confederate veterans were still in the land of the living. Before the speaking, the Daughters of the Confederacy provided them with a bountiful barbecue on the courthouse square. Others added to their pleasure by bringing a supply of moonshine from the Catfish section of Catawba County.

"After the eating and the drinking, the old soldiers repaired to the auditorium in the courthouse, and I delivered my speech, which I had prepared with meticulous care. An old soldier who sat on the front bench gave me the most rapt attention I have ever received from any member of an audience. He seemed to hang on every word I uttered.

"I reached the climax of my speech. I said, 'I saw you undergo your baptism of blood at Bethel, I saw you storm Cemetery Ridge at Gettysburg, I saw you fight the Battle above the Clouds on Lookout Mountain.' At this juncture the most attentive member of the audience staggered to his feet and shouted, 'That's a damned lie. You weren't there.'

"I lost my composure completely, and had the greatest difficulty regaining it."

❧   Two of the most gallant of Burke County's fifteen hundred Confederate soldiers were Joe Allman and his younger brother, Noah, who were affectionately known by the community as Uncle Joe and Uncle Noah. They served in one of North Carolina's most heroic combat units, the famous Sixth North Carolina Regiment. Uncle

Noah was a teetotalist, but Uncle Joe sometimes succumbed to the temptation to imbibe a little too freely.

Uncle Joe's devotion to the Confederacy intensified as the years passed. He attended all reunions of Confederate veterans, arrayed with the badges and ribbons denoting his attendance at previous reunions.

Shortly after our wedding trip, my wife and I met Uncle Joe on a Morganton sidewalk. He was en route to the forthcoming reunion in Memphis, bedecked with all his badges and ribbons. Uncle Joe extracted a bottle of booze from his hip pocket and invited my wife and me to drink with him.

At that time North Carolina was bedeviled by the hysteria of prohibition, and the courts rarely extended any mercy to anyone who was apprehended in the possession of intoxicating beverages. In declining his invitation, I gave Uncle Joe this warning, "Uncle Joe, please put that bottle back in your pocket. If the police catch you with it, they will take you to jail, and you'll miss the reunion."

"Don't you worry about that," Uncle Joe said. "Before the police could even lock the jailhouse door, Sue Tate and the Daughters of the Confederacy would set me free and send me to Memphis."

Knowing Cousin Sue as I did, I am convinced that Uncle Joe was right.

After the Good Lord called Uncle Joe hence, a former resident visited Morganton, met Uncle Noah, and asked him about Uncle Joe. "Brother Joe died last year," Uncle Noah informed him. "If he hadn't drunk so much mean booze, he might have lived to a ripe old age."

"How old was Uncle Joe when he died?" the former resident inquired.

Uncle Noah replied, "About ninety."

❧ The Morganton chapter of the Daughters of the Confederacy had been named the Colonel Samuel McDowell Tate Chapter in honor of Cousin Sue Tate's father, who had led the Sixth North Carolina Regiment with intrepidity at Gettysburg.

Cousin Sue served as the perennial chairwoman of the program committee of the chapter. She made it a practice to postpone arranging a program for a meeting of the chapter until just before the meeting was scheduled to be held. One Monday night about midnight, Cousin Sue called me and extended to me an invitation to speak to the Daughters of the Confederacy on the subject of Jefferson Davis at a dinner meeting on the following evening.

I told Cousin Sue I could not accept her invitation. I had spent all of Monday in court trying a case, I would have to spend all day Tuesday doing the same thing, and I would not have any opportunity to think what I should say about Jefferson Davis.

Cousin Sue replied, "I won't take no for an answer. Any good Southerner ought to be able to make a speech on Jefferson Davis at any time, in any place, and on any occasion without any preparation. Besides, you don't need any time to think what you should say about Jefferson Davis. I've heard you speak, and I know you speak without thinking."

I made the speech.

During the centennial of the Civil War, organizations known as Civil War Roundtables sprang up throughout the land to memorialize the glory and sacrifice of both the North and the South.

With my good friend and senatorial aide Harry Gatton, I joined the Washington Civil War Roundtable, whose members were divided almost equally between those of Northern and those of Southern antecedents.

The Washington Roundtable occasionally held dinner meetings in the evening. Although it did not precede these meetings with cocktail parties, it did permit caterers to set up bars and assuage the thirst of its members.

On one occasion I accepted an invitation to speak to a dinner meeting of the Washington Roundtable upon a subject of my choice. I spoke on the religious faith of Abraham Lincoln.

As an American history buff, I enshrine Lincoln among America's greatest. Although he did not formally accept membership in any church, Lincoln was a deeply religious person. He is quoted as having said that the perplexities of the presidency during the Civil War often drove him to his knees in prayer because he had no other place to go.

In pessimistic moments, I am tempted to surmise that Lincoln may owe his historical immortality to the good fortune of having lived and died when he did. History indicates that his father, Thomas Lincoln, was something of a ne'er-do-well. If Lincoln had lived nowadays, the federal government might have put Thomas on relief, and Abraham might have turned out to be as worthless as a tinker's damn.

  On the evening before my speech, I met Ulysses S. Grant III, grandson of the original Ulysses S. Grant and member of the Washington Roundtable, who had retired to private life after distinguished service as a general in the Army's Engineering Corps and a commissioner of the District of Columbia.

I invited General Grant to have a drink with me. He replied somewhat humorously that he did not know whether he ought to accept my invitation. I thereupon said to him, "Your grandfather did more to restore love for the Union in Southern hearts than anyone else when he paroled General Lee and his men at Appomattox upon the simple condition that they obey the laws and permitted them to return to their homes in freedom with their sidearms and horses. Besides, he revealed the goodness of his heart by ordering each Union soldier who had more than one ration to give his extra ration to a Confederate. The Confederates had been subsisting in large measure for many days on parched corn and buds of tree leaves, and were on the verge of starvation. I had great uncles who surrendered with Lee at Appomattox, and were benefited by your grandfather's wisdom and goodness. Since he is not here to accept my gratitude, I ask you to act as his proxy, and have a drink with me."

General Grant said, "I accept your invitation with pleasure."

  Some weeks later Harry Gatton and I journeyed with other members of the Washington Roundtable by bus to visit the battlefield at Brandy Station, Virginia. On our arrival, Colonel Seaborne, a retired army officer, who had made a protracted study of the battle, gave us a guided tour of the battlefield.

He told us in an illuminating way how General Jeb Stuart, the commander of the Confederate cavalry, who loved the pageantry of war, had staged a colorful parade and review the day before the battle. Later, he had unwisely bivouacked the artillery between the cavalry and the infantry and the Rappahannock River for the ensuing night, and General Alfred Pleasonton, commander of the Union cavalry, had crossed the Rappahannock at Beverly Ford before daybreak on the day of the battle and surprised and almost defeated General Stuart before he could rally his men.

After our tour of the battlefield, the members of the Washington Roundtable lunched at Brandy Station. Just before the lunch ended, Colonel Seaborne told me that I was the only member of Congress present, and he would like to call on me for some remarks as soon as the lunch ended. I advised him that although I did not have any notion of what I would say, I would be glad to speak. When Colonel Seaborne presented me, I made these remarks:

"Colonel Seaborne has given us a most illuminating description of the Battle of Brandy Station. General Pleasonton's action in crossing the river at Beverly Ford before daybreak—a time when all the God-fearing and law-abiding ought to have been sleeping—discloses what General Bob Toombs of Georgia meant when he said you couldn't count on Yankees to do the reasonable thing.

"Senator Dick Russell, of Georgia, an American history buff, tells an intriguing story about Bob Toombs, a distinguished Georgia politician, who served as a general in the armies of the Confederacy during what Collier Cobb, my professor of geology at Chapel Hill, habitually called the 'Uncivil War.'

"Bob Toombs, so Senator Russell says, was an ardent secessionist. He urged Georgia to secede and join her sister Southern states in the Confederacy. He assured Georgia that the Yankees would not do anything to prevent such action, and that if they did, the Confederacy could beat them with cornstalks.

"All of you Civil War buffs know what happened. According to Senator Russell's story, Toombs refrained from becoming a candidate for any public office until he was satisfied Georgians had forgotten his optimistic, but erroneous, assurance about what would happen if they seceded.

"After a substantial time, Toombs sought a public office. When he was speaking for his candidacy in a Georgia courthouse, a member of the audience, who was wearing a tattered Confederate uniform and who had a patch over his right eye, an empty right sleeve, and a peg leg, arose and put this inquiry to him: 'General Toombs, didn't you tell us that the Yankees wouldn't do anything to prevent secession, and that if they did we could beat them with cornstalks?'

"According to Senator Russell, General Toombs replied, 'I did. But it happened that the Yankees wouldn't do the reasonable thing. They wouldn't fight with cornstalks.'

"I like to meditate on the great ifs of history. All Civil War buffs know that the South wore itself out trying to beat the Yankees. Suppose the South had beat the Yankees just before it wore itself out trying to do that. In other words, suppose secession had been a success rather than a failure.

"In that event, the South would now be an independent foreign nation; most of the Northern States would be seeking to secede and join her; and if the South cast a single furtive look in the direction of Moscow, Secretary of State John Foster Dulles would be running down here and begging us to accept millions and millions of dollars of foreign aid."

❦ I served in France with Company I of the Twenty-Eighth Infantry, a unit of the First Division, during the First World War. Brigadier General Beaumont B. Buck, our brigade commander, delighted to narrate this story:

"When Congress declared war on Germany, I was stationed at Fort Ringgold, Texas. I had a little patch of earth enclosed by a fence behind my quarters, and I donned old army fatigues and raised flowers and vegetables in it in my moments of leisure.

"After the declaration of war, the army's ranks were swelled by untrained recruits. While I was digging in the little patch of earth behind my quarters, two recruits came by, leaned on the fence, and asked me for matches to light their cigarettes. After complying with their requests, I asked them how long they had been in the army. They replied about a week. I asked them how they liked the army. They said they liked everything and everybody except the fellow who was called Sergeant. They said they didn't like him at all.

"One of them asked me whether I was in the army. On receiving my affirmative answer, he asked me how long I had been in the army. I told him some thirty years. He said that I must be a sergeant. I told him I was not a sergeant. He said that I must be a corporal. I told him I was not a corporal.

"He looked at me right hard, and said, 'Mister, if you've been in the army thirty years and are not a sergeant or a corporal, you must be mighty dumb.'"

❦ Lieutenant Robert O. Purdy, who made the supreme sacrifice at Soissons in July, 1918, had an engaging sense of humor. He was commander of the guard one dark night at a French village behind the front where the Third Battalion of the Twenty-Eighth Infantry was billeted. As he was visiting the various posts and inspecting the guards at them, he heard someone approaching through the darkness.

Lieutenant Purdy sang out, "Who goes there?" The voice of an obviously inebriated man responded, "One drunk soldier and three bottles of champagne." Lieutenant Purdy responded, "Advance drunken soldier and three bottles of champagne."

When the soldier reached the guard post, Lieutenant Purdy relieved him of one bottle of champagne. After reimbursing the soldier for its cost, the lieutenant ordered, "Pass drunken soldier and two bottles of champagne." The soldier staggered on his merry way with the other bottles.

❦ Humor reveals itself at times in strange places and in strange ways. About daybreak on May 28, 1918, the Twenty-Eighth Infantry went "over the top" at Cantigny, France, in the first American battle of the First World War. An improvised field hospital had been set up in a large dugout under the chalk cliffs near the jumping-off place.

After a time American medical corpsmen brought a badly wounded American boy into the dugout on a stretcher. A medical officer examined the wounded boy and realized he was beyond the help of medicine or surgery. As he lay dying, the boy smiled and said, "Well Doc, this is one time you'll not give me a c.c. pill and mark me 'duty.'"

Sometime later Company I and other combat units of the Twenty-Eighth Infantry were entrenched in a nearby area where substantial deposits of chalk lay just below the earth's surface. Inasmuch as the trenches had just been dug, the chalk exposed at the time of their digging marked the location of the trenches with precision and made them vivid targets for the German artillery on moonlit nights.

Because of the intensity of the German shelling of the area at all times, the mess sergeant of Company I was able to send food, which was always slum-gullion, to his entrenched comrades only once during a twenty-four-hour period. The detachment that brought the food usually reached the entrenched men about midnight.

Just after the slum-gullion had been poured into the mess kits of the entrenched men and they were partaking of their only meal of the day, the German artillery bombarded the trenches with great intensity. An exploding shell hurled into the air a mass of dirt and chalk, much of which fell into the mess kit of Private Williams, a native of Pennsylvania.

Williams was one of the world's worst stutterers, and ordinarily had much difficulty expressing himself in understandable fashion. When he realized he would not have any food except cold hardtack for another twenty-four hours, Williams temporarily lost his impediment of speech and cursed the Germans and his own sad fate with fiery fluency.

After a few moments, however, he subsided with the philosophical observation, "Well, this won't matter fifty years from now."

This bit of philosophy has stood me in good stead during the intervening years. After all, what seems to be of crucial import today may be of little consequence tomorrow.

❦   Those who serve in a combat unit in war experience more pathos than humor.

Sam Cornew, mess sergeant of Company I, was a monster of a man in size. He must have weighed three hundred pounds if he weighed an ounce. Anyone who was not intimately acquainted with Sam was apt to conclude he was a monster in other respects, for he usually revealed about as much compassion as a meat axe. He railed at everybody in sight and hurled foul epithets at his cooks and kitchen police. But Sam Cornew had a heart of gold.

When he learned that the First Division was being withdrawn for rest and replenishment after five days of desperate fighting at Soissons in the beginning of the Aisne-Marne offensive, Sam and his cooks and kitchen police prepared a feast for the survivors of Company I.

He walked toward Soissons to greet the survivors and tell them of the feast that was awaiting them. Company I had entered the battle with about 180 officers and men. When he met the 38 battle-weary and unwounded survivors, Sam sat down by the roadside and wept with the abandon of a grieving child.

Of the men assigned to Company I during the First World War, 79 died in battle, and virtually all the others suffered one or more wounds. The losses of the other combat units of the Twenty-Eighth Infantry and the First Division were appalling.

After the fight at Cantigny, Marshal Pétain, commander in chief of the French Armies, cited the Twenty-Eighth Infantry in army orders in these words: "A regiment inspired by a magnificent offensive spirit. On the 28th of May, 1918, under command of Colonel H. E. Ely, this regiment rushed forward with irresistible dash to attack a strongly fortified village. It reached all of its objectives, and held the conquered ground in spite of repeated counterattacks."

I treasure in my memory with profound affection and admiration those who served in Company I. I reserve the softest spot, however, for Corporal Arlie C. Oppenheim and Private Dewey Price. They and I were the three survivors of the six men who silenced a German machine gun which was pouring a deadly hail of bullets into the Twenty-Eighth Infantry at Soissons.

In after years, Arlie visited my home in Morganton. I was recuperating from a recent operation for appendicitis, and my wife, who still tries to laugh at my jokes after fifty-eight years, was most solicitous in her care of me.

Arlie said, "Miss Margaret, I don't want to criticize such a lovely lady as you. But I'm compelled to protest the way you're treating my old comrade. You're making a pansy of him."

❧ While serving as colonel in the American Military Police in Germany during the Second World War, Doggie Hatcher captured Franz von Papen, whom William L. Shirer has described in *The Rise and Fall of the Third Reich* as the German most responsible for Adolf Hitler's rise to power. Pictures of Doggie Hatcher and his captive appeared in the national press.

After the Second World War had ended and Doggie appeared once more at his favorite civic club, the Morganton Kiwanis Club, Carl Wonner, who was known for his wit, arose and told the Kiwanians he was going to reveal the truth about the capture of von Papen.

Von Papen, he said, was actually captured by a private, who did not know what he should do with his notorious prisoner. The private sent for the corporal; the corporal sent for the sergeant; the sergeant sent for the lieutenant; the lieutenant sent for the captain; the captain sent for the major; the major sent for Colonel Hatcher; and Colonel Hatcher sent for the photographer.

❧ Accompanied by my wife, I visited some of our military and naval installations in England, Scotland, Denmark, West Germany, France, Italy, Spain, and Portugal in late November, 1965, under the auspices of the Senate Armed Services Committee. We had many delightful and enlightening experiences. One of the most enjoyable of them was our visit to Heidelberg, where we attended at the invitation of Brigadier General Robert M. Williams the banquet which American military lawyers in West Germany hold each year to honor the civilian judges of West Germany. General Williams, the chief of the Judge Advocate General's Corps in West Germany, had conceived the idea of holding the banquet to strengthen understanding between America and West Germany several years before.

On his arrival in West Germany he had wanted to become proficient in writing and speaking German. He employed a German tutor, and studied the language diligently under his instruction. While the first banquet was in the planning stage, the notion occurred to him that it would be appropriate for him to make a statement in German welcoming the German judges to the banquet. He wrote a welcoming statement in German, memorized it, and rehearsed it before his German tutor. He refrained from using the statement, however, on getting this advice from his tutor: "If I were you, I'd extend a welcome to the German judges in English and let a competent intermediary interpret it to them. If you were to make a welcoming speech in German in conformity with your script, few of the American military lawyers, and none of the German judges, would understand it."

Chapter 5

Humor in Politics

 ❧ ❧ ❧

When he was the Democratic nominee for vice-president in 1928, Senator Joseph T. Robinson, of Arkansas, spoke at Charlotte. "Politics is not a vocation," he said. "It is not even an avocation. It's an incurable disease. If it ever gets in one's blood, it can never be eradicated."

I was born to a family whose blood had been corrupted by politics. My forebears had been immersed in law and politics for generations. I will not climb my family tree to prove this statement. That would entail the risk of finding some horse thieves hanging on some of the branches.

I nevertheless confess that genealogy is fascinating to me. It teaches the truth that William Cullen Bryant enunciates in his poem "Thanatopsis," namely, that they who tread the globe are but a handful to the tribes who slumber in its bosom.

On rare occasions research in genealogy unearths amusing incidents. Some of my ancestors lived and died in New England before the Revolution. When I did some research concerning them, I found an incident relating to one of them in the annals of Massachusetts. It indicates that he was Yankee to the bone in thriftiness. The record solemnly discloses that he was a joiner, or carpenter, by trade, that he made a coffin for himself, and that he used it as a "chist" for the storage of apples until he "dyed and used it himself."

❧ My New England ancestors moved to Nantucket, became members of the Society of Friends, and joined the Quaker migration to the present North Carolina counties of Guilford and Randolph just before the Revolution.

I have been privileged to make the commencement address on two occasions at Guilford College, the great institution of learning founded and maintained by North Carolina Quakers. At one of them, I was introduced by a distant relative, Robert Frazier, chairman of the college board of trustees. He told the audience I was descended from the Quaker family that bears the surname Coffin.

At the beginning of my remarks, I stated that I was also a descendant of Quaker families bearing the surnames Bunker, Folger, Gardner, Gorham, Hussey, Macy, Starbuck, and Worth, and was collaterally related to the Hobbs and Mendenhall families. On the conclusion of the commencement exercises, a substantial part of the audience assured me that they were my relatives if I had told them the truth about my Quaker antecedents.

❦ Despite my disinclination to climb my family tree, I will make some comments on my great-great-grandfather Joseph Wilson, a disciple of Thomas Jefferson, who served three terms in the North Carolina House of Commons shortly after 1800 and a quarter of a century as solicitor or district attorney of the vast judicial district that stretched from Mecklenburg County on the east through what is now Cherokee County on the west.

Each of us is said to be the product of heredity and environment. If this be true, I may have inherited some of my love for humor and frankness from Joseph Wilson.

As chairman of a committee of the House of Commons charged with responsibility for preparing a plan to redistrict North Carolina's congressional districts after the census of 1800, Joseph presented to the House a bill implementing the committee's assignment. A Federalist member challenged the fairness of the bill on the ground that it gerrymandered the districts to insure the election to Congress of Jeffersonians. By way of pleading guilty to this soft impeachment, Joseph said, "That was our objective. If the gentleman can suggest how the House can achieve our objective with greater certainty, I'll offer amendments conforming to his suggestions."

❦ While Joseph Wilson was serving as solicitor, counterfeiting was rife in Western North Carolina, and the responsibility for bringing the counterfeiters to justice devolved on him. On one occasion he persuaded the jury to convict a notorious counterfeiter, and the presiding judge sentenced the counterfeiter to pay an enormous fine. After the counterfeiter had paid the fine and left for parts unknown, it was discovered that he had paid it in counterfeit money.

Joseph may not have seen anything humorous in that event. But he afterward injected a little humor into the most solemn document he ever executed, namely, his will, which appears of record in the office of the clerk of the superior court of Mecklenburg County. In it, he stipulated, in essence, "If I should have any property at the time of my death, which I most seriously doubt will be the case, I bequeath and devise it to my beloved wife."

❧ Samuel P. Carson, of Burke County, represented the Western North Carolina District in Congress from 1825 until 1831. While history records the events I discuss, I base my recital of them in large measure on oral traditions.

Inasmuch as no man lives or dies to himself, the story of Sam Carson necessitates reference to his predecessor in Congress, Dr. Robert Brank Vance, and Dr. Vance's predecessor in Congress, Felix Walker.

Felix Walker, a hero of the Revolutionary and Indian Wars, was a colorful politician. His suavity earned for him the sobriquet "Old Oil Jug." After filling many other offices, he represented the Western North Carolina District in Congress from 1817 to 1823. He is known to fame for adding to the language the word *buncombe* as a synonym for insincere speech made by a politician merely to please his constituents.

On one occasion, Walker delivered a protracted speech against a bill whose passage by the United States House of Representatives was a foregone conclusion. On being asked by an impatient colleague why he persisted in speaking, Walker replied, "I'm talking for Buncombe," naming one of the counties in his district.

Dr. Vance, an uncle of the famous Zeb Vance, defeated Walker by one vote in 1822 and served in the House from 1823 until 1825. He was defeated by Carson in 1824 and again in 1826. Embittered by his defeat, he asserted that Carson's aged father had taken British protection during the Revolution. Under the cruel code duello, which

prevailed among politicians of the day, Carson was virtually compelled to challenge Dr. Vance to a duel. Prior to their meeting at
Saluda Gap, South Carolina, on November 20, 1827, Carson's friend
the famous David Crockett instructed him in the use of pistols.

Carson mortally wounded Dr. Vance, who was removed to a nearby
tavern. As he was dying, Vance, who had been a constant reader of
Shakespeare, quoted these melancholy words of Macbeth:

> To-morrow, and to-morrow, and to-morrow,
> Creeps in this petty pace from day to day,
> To the last syllable of recorded time;
> And all our yesterdays have lighted fools
> The way to dusty death. Out, out, brief candle!
> Life's but a walking shadow, a poor player
> That struts and frets his hour upon the stage
> And then is heard no more: it is a tale
> Told by an idiot, full of sound and fury,
> Signifying nothing.

❦　I digress from the Carson story to tell how Burton Craige, who
was one of North Carolina's finest public servants, employed his
sense of humor in later years to ridicule the code duello.

A diminutive editor, who was less than five feet and a half in
height, challenged Craige, who was almost seven feet tall, to a duel.
Craige wrote the editor a note stating, in substance, "I accept your
challenge. Since the code duello empowers the challenged party to
designate the weapons and place of combat, I hereby name broad-
swords as the weapons, and a spot in the Yadkin River where the
water is six feet deep as the place of combat." On receipt of Craige's
note, the editor withdrew his challenge.

❦　Carson was much saddened in after years by the memory of his
duel with Vance. Subsequent to that tragic event, he was opposed
for reelection by David Newland, who was not a profound literary
scholar.

Newland persuaded one of Carson's political enemies, Samuel
Hillman, an erudite member of the Morganton bar, to write a cam-

paign speech for him. The Hillman production abounded in literary gems. For example, the script referred to an unfulfilled promise made by Carson in a previous campaign and averred that the promise was sleeping in the tomb of the Capulets.

Newland memorized the Hillman manuscript and employed it as a campaign speech in a debate with Carson, who was not averse to indulging in a little demagoguery. In replying to Newland, Carson said changed circumstances had made his prior promise inappropriate. He added, "I thought I knew everybody who has lived in this district during my lifetime, and the locations of the burial places of such of them as have died. I've never heard of Mr. Capulet or the place of his burial. I am compelled to call on my opponent for enlightenment. Pray tell me, Mr. Newland, where Mr. Capulet lived, and where his grave can be found."

Inasmuch as he knew nothing about Romeo and Juliet, Newland was unable to enlighten Carson.

As a congressman, Carson supported John C. Calhoun's doctrine of nullification. Some of his constituents who abhorred nullification arranged a meeting in the only structure in Morganton large enough to house a public gathering of the contemplated size, namely, the Presbyterian church, to condemn Carson's espousal of nullification. Samuel Hillman was scheduled to make the condemnatory speech and propose a motion of censure.

According to the custom of the day, a large decanter of white brandy was placed on the table assigned to the speaker. To the surprise of those present, Carson entered the meeting just before it was to begin and demanded equal time with Hillman. As a matter of fairness, Carson was accorded equal time on condition he spoke first and Hillman replied to him.

From time to time during his protracted remarks, Carson poured copious amounts of the white brandy into two glasses, handed one of the glasses to Hillman, who drained its contents, and pretended to drink from the other. By the time Carson ended his speech, Hillman was too inebriated to arise. In consequence, no condemnatory speech was made, and no motion to censure was proposed.

Carson was defeated for reelection to Congress. Afterward he served in the State Senate in 1834 and the North Carolina constitutional convention of 1835. He then removed to Texas and became secretary of state of the Lone Star Republic.

❧   I am indebted to Uncle Billy Hallyburton for a marvelous story about an event of the late 1880s or early 1890s. At that time Burke County people received most of their amusement, information, misinformation, and inspiration by attending court, political gatherings, and churches. Often political speeches and sermons were hours in length.

One Saturday, Judge Darius H. Starbuck, a Republican of no mean oratorical ability, harangued Burke County Republicans at the old Burke County Stone Courthouse for several hours, charging the Democratic Party with massive corruption and rascality. The speech had a depressing effect on local Democratic leaders. They begged their oratorical idol, Zeb Vance, who was to speak at the same place the ensuing Saturday, to say something to counteract Judge Starbuck's remarks. Vance answered their plea.

During the course of his two-hour speech, Vance said, "Fellow Democrats, I understand Judge Starbuck, who is not much of a star but is a hell of a buck, heaped some red coals of fire on us Democrats last Saturday. I know Judge Starbuck well. Despite his vicious assertions concerning us, he is not really mean at heart. He's just ignorant, and doesn't know what he talks about.

"In fact," Vance continued, "Judge Starbuck is the most ignorant man I've ever known, except a half-wit I met in a cove in Madison County in 1876 when I was running against Judge Thomas Settle, a really intelligent Republican, for the governorship of North Carolina. Being unacquainted with the half-wit's mental state, I asked him whether he supported Vance or Settle for governor, and he gave me a blank stare, and asked, 'What is Vance? What is Settle? What is governor?'

I then attempted to explain to him," Vance said, "that Vance and Settle were opposing candidates for governor of North Carolina. He inquired, 'What is North Carolina?' I then asked the half-wit whether he had ever heard of George Washington or the Twelve Apostles. He answered these questions in the negative. I then put this inquiry to him: 'Have you ever heard of God?' For the first time a faint glimmer of intelligence appeared in the half-wit's eyes, and he said, 'It seems like I have. His last name is Damn, ain't it?' "

Vance ended his comments on this subject with this assurance: "Fellow Democrats, Judge Starbuck is the most ignorant man I've ever known other than that Madison County idiot."

🐱 Uncle Jimmy Mull was the bellwether of the Democrats residing in the Fiddler's Run neighborhood of Burke County. They sent him to Morganton in 1884 to ascertain how the three Democratic leaders of Burke County—Judge Alphonso C. Avery, Major James W. Wilson, and Colonel Samuel McDowell Tate—wanted them to vote in the statewide referendum on prohibition. When he reported to them, Uncle Jimmy said, "Boys, we're going to have to decide this for ourselves. The Judge air fur prohibition; the Major air agin it; and the Colonel air mutual [neutral]."

Prohibition was defeated in the referendum, probably because most of the voters entertained attitudes similar to that of Zeb Vance. When the Reverend Robert Laban Abernethy urged Vance to support prohibition in the referendum, Vance replied, "Abernethy, my heart is with you, but my thirst is against you."

🐱 The most unforgivable litigation in Western North Carolina is a law suit involving a disputed boundary line. Uncle Jimmy Mull and Bartlett A. Berry owned adjoining farms and became involved in a law suit in respect to the location of the dividing line between them. Tradition does not inform us as to what the decision in the law suit was, but it does tell us that it produced years of dislike and silence between the litigants.

After about ten years, Uncle Jimmy was plowing near the disputed boundary line. Bart Berry approached him, and said, "Morning, Jimmy." Jimmy asked, "What do you mean speaking to me after these years of silence?" Bart replied, "I've just come to tell you I'm going to run for sheriff this fall on the Democratic ticket, and I don't want you or any of your folks to vote for me." Jimmy responded, "Me and my folks have been voting the straight Democratic ticket ever since Andy Jackson ran for president. If you don't want me and my folks to vote for you, you'll have to keep your damned name off the Democratic ballot."

❧   Joseph Spainhour, of the Morganton bar, was an able advocate before juries, a civic and political leader, and a devoted churchman. He sometimes assumed political positions inconsistent with those he had taken in times past. Nobody could put him on the defensive because of these inconsistencies. He airily dismissed them with the assertion, "Maybe I was wrong then, but I'm right now."

Spainhour and Mose Harshaw were captivating political speakers. In 1898 they were, respectively, the Democratic and Republican candidates for the office of solicitor of their judicial district. They met in joint debate at the village of Chesterfield in Burke County.

Spainhour, who spoke first, said, "My opponent, Mose N. Harshaw, is not the illustrious Moses of the Bible. He's plain old Mose Harshaw who was born and reared at Globe in Caldwell County."

By way of reply, Mose Harshaw said, "Like Brother Spainhour said, 'I'm not the Moses of the Bible. I'm just plain old Mose Harshaw of Caldwell County.' In one respect, however, Joe Spainhour reminds me of the Joseph of the Bible. Joe Spainhour was rocked in a Democratic cradle and nourished at a Democratic table. Four years ago, however, he forsook the Democratic Party, accepted the nomination of the Populists for solicitor of this district, sought and secured the endorsement of the Republicans, and defeated that faithful Democrat Will Newland, of Lenoir, who was the nominee of the party which Joe had deserted. After the Populists vanished from the political landscape and the Republicans gave me instead of him their nomination for the solicitorship, he returned to the household of his original political faith, and the Democrats received him as a Prodigal Son and gave him their nomination. Because of his spotted public career, I am bound to admit that in one respect Joe Spainhour resembles the Joseph of the Bible. He wears a coat of many political colors."

❧   Robert O. Huffman, of Morganton, was one of North Carolina's most enlightened industrialists. As a citizen of broad interests, he enjoyed discussing virtually all things under the sun with all friends; and as a staunch Republican, he relished poking fun at his Democratic friends, of whom I was privileged to be one.

During my youthful days near the end of the Woodrow Wilson administration, I met Rob and told him I had been reading Mark Twain and had much appreciated his books *A Tramp Abroad* and *Pudd'nhead Wilson*. Rob observed, "I knew Pudd'nhead Wilson was President, but I had no idea Mark Twain had written a book about him."

Like many other of my Republican friends, Rob voted for me when I ran for office. He justified his political apostasy by saying he was a "Sam Ervin Republican."

꽃 When Governor Alfred E. Smith, of New York, was the Democratic presidential nominee in 1928, I supported his candidacy with much enthusiasm. I believed the election of a Catholic to the presidency would fulfill in a fine way the constitutional pledge that "no religious test shall ever be required as a qualification to any office or public trust under the United States." I also believed that, like Grover Cleveland, he was a man of rugged integrity, and was well equipped by common sense and courage to make a great president.

My enthusiasm was shared by my small son, Sam Ervin III, despite the fact that he was then less than three years of age. He had shaken hands with Al Smith when his train passed through Morganton and was always ready to doff his little brown derby and speak in behalf of Smith's candidacy. Both of us were distressed when Herbert Hoover crushed Al Smith and all Democratic candidates in our area of North Carolina went down to defeat.

Shortly afterward, William Vroman, a jocular Republican, Joseph H. Buckley, a loyal Democrat, and I were elected deacons in the Presbyterian church. My grief in respect to the recent presidential election was substantially alleviated by an observation of Bill Vroman's. As we were walking down the church aisle to be ordained and installed in our solemn ecclesiastical offices, Bill whispered in my ear, "You and Joe Buckley are the only Al Smith Democrats who got elected to anything this fall."

The grief of Sam Ervin III vanished completely when Christmas came. As the only child at the time in our family connections and the neighborhood, relatives, neighbors, and Santa Claus heaped gifts on him. As he surveyed their largess with joy on Christmas morning, he revealed his precocious political acumen by this remark to his parents: "We'll run Santa Claus for president next time. Nobody will vote against him."

❦   During its 1931 session, the General Assembly of North Carolina, which was considering bills to reorganize state government, invited Al Smith, a visitor to Pinehurst, who had done noteworthy work in that field as governor of New York, to address it on the subject. The General Assembly sent a committee to Pinehurst to extend its invitation to Al Smith, who accepted it.

After he had accepted the invitation, Will Woodard, a member of the committee, stated to Al Smith, "If it hadn't been for your religion, you would have been president." Al Smith replied, 'I'd hate to believe that. I'll have to admit, however, that many voters seemed to believe that the pope would take over the country if I should be elected. I don't believe the pope wants to do that. If he had entertained that desire, he could have bought the country right cheap from the Harding administration during Teapot Dome days."

❦   Frank D. Grist, the representative from Caldwell County, and I occupied adjoining seats in the 1923 session of the North Carolina House. Both of us had served in the First Division in the First World War, and Frank had been seriously wounded in action. We formed an enduring friendship. Frank received a petition signed by the pastor and congregation of a small country church which urged him to secure the passage of a bill "repealing all the loopholes in the law." Frank presented the petition to me with this tongue-in-cheek request: "I'm not a lawyer. So I ask you to draft the bill for me." I had to confess that I did not know exactly what a legal loophole was, and for that reason was unable to draft the bill.

❦   Frank Grist was subsequently elected North Carolina's commissioner of labor and printing, and altogether served in that post with great ability for eight years.

After Senator Lee S. Overman died in office in 1930, a Democratic primary was held in North Carolina to name a candidate for the unexpired remainder of his term. Several persons, including Frank Grist, qualified as candidates in this primary. For a reason I cannot fathom an editorial writer of the *Greensboro Daily News* had taken a strong dislike to Frank. He wrote a scathing editorial against his candidacy in which he said that "Frank Grist is not qualified to be a dog-catcher."

On the advice of his attorney, Frank sent a telegram to the *News* threatening a libel suit against it unless it retracted the editorial. The editorial writer wrote a second editorial which added insult to injury. The editorial stated, in effect, that the *News* did not wish to be sued and for that reason would retract its statement that Frank Grist was not fit to be a dog-catcher. It added, in substance, that in order to make its retraction complete, the *News* would say that "Frank Grist is fit to be a dog-catcher, but instead of running for that office he is seeking the post of United States Senator."

There were a number of candidates in the first North Carolina Democratic gubernatorial primary in 1936. It was recognized that neither of the two leading candidates, Clyde R. Hoey or Doctor McDonald, would obtain a majority vote and that a second, or run-off, primary between them would be necessary to determine the nominee. I was managing the campaign for Hoey in Burke County and was relying on my good friend Walter Giles to look after his interests in Big Silver Creek Precinct, where Earle Butler was Doctor McDonald's manager.

At that time state law required the precinct election officials to open absentee ballots and deposit them in the ballot boxes with other ballots at three o'clock in the afternoon. The polls closed at sunset.

After the polls had closed and the precinct election officials were counting the ballots, Giles called me by telephone. He gave me the following information in an agitated voice.

As three o'clock approached, voting in Big Silver Creek was very heavy. Butler said the precinct election officials ought not to delay those who were voting in person by opening the absentee ballots and putting them in the boxes at that time. Giles agreed. At their joint request, the precinct officials agreed to postpone doing these things until the polls closed and they began counting the votes.

When they undertook to do this, it appeared that there was one tow sack filled with absentee ballots for McDonald and two tow sacks filled with absentee ballots for Hoey. On learning this, Butler challenged the validity of all the absentee ballots on the ground that they had not been opened and deposited in the boxes at three o'clock in conformity to law.

I said, "Walt, I don't see how so many absentee ballots could have been obtained in Big Silver Creek without bending the election laws. There's going to be a run-off primary, and we do not want any scandal to arise concerning any votes for Hoey. I advise you to urge the precinct officials to sustain Butler's challenge and reject all of the absentee ballots."

An irritated Walt Giles responded, "You're a damn fool advising that all these absentee ballots be thrown away. Besides, some of them are legal."

🦋 Richard Brevard Russell, long-time senator from Georgia, was ideally equipped in all respects for the presidency of the United States. If he had been born and lived in Kalamazoo, Michigan, instead of Winder, Georgia, he might have been called to that high office.

During his time, however, it was easier for a rich man to travel through a needle's eye than it was for a Southerner who was faithful to the traditions of the South to obtain the presidential nomination of a major political party. Nevertheless, Senator Russell became a prospective candidate in 1952, and his candidacy was supported by Northern as well as Southern Democrats in the convention which sat at Chicago.

At that time a researcher in history in Mecklenburg County, North Carolina, dug up some data indicating that Russell and Adlai E. Stevenson, of Illinois, who was the leading contender for the Democratic presidential nomination, were both descended from Richard Brevard, a revolutionary patriot of Mecklenburg County.

On being asked by a reporter about this, Russell said, "I'm not denying my kinship to any Democrat at this time."

❧ I now undertake to relate an entrancing story which Thruston Morton, a colleague in the Senate, told me concerning his fellow Kentuckian John Sherman Cooper. Insofar as my fallible memory permits, I will try to repeat it as he told it to me.

Shortly after President Eisenhower's inauguration, John Sherman Cooper, a much-beloved and respected member of the Senate, received a letter from his old friend George, who resided with his wife, Mandy, on a little rocky farm at Sleepy Hollow, Kentucky.

"Dear John Sherman," George wrote. "As you know I've always been a loyal Republican, and one of your staunch supporters. Mandy and I are growing older, and our arthritis is becoming more painful day by day. We're having a hard time eking out a living on our little rocky farm. I've decided to ask you to get me a government job. I've already picked out the job I want. It is ambassador to the Court of St. James. I'm sure President Eisenhower will give me that job if you'll go to the White House and ask him to do so. I'm counting on you."

Senator Cooper transmitted George's letter to Thruston Morton, who was then serving as an assistant secretary of state. He requested Thruston to persuade some highly skilled diplomat in the State Department to prepare for him a reply to George which would reveal the crucial importance of the ambassadorship to the Court of St. James without giving offense to his old friend. Thruston returned the letter to Senator Cooper with the statement that no diplomat in the State Department possessed sufficient skill to compose an appropriate reply and that he would have to perform that task himself.

Senator Cooper thereupon drafted a reply which illustrated the mastery of diplomacy he subsequently exhibited as ambassador to India and East Germany.

"Dear George," he said. "The Republican Party owes you any office within its gift, and I'll be glad to help you obtain any office you want. As your friend, however, I want to warn you that being ambassador to the Court of St. James isn't always a bed of roses. I'm going to tell you about some of its drawbacks. I suggest that you talk about them with Mandy, and advise me later whether the ambassador to the Court of St. James is your final choice. The ambassador to the Court of St. James can't get much rest in the daylight hours because he is annoyed all day by trivial demands of Americans visiting England, and he can't get much sleep at night because he lies awake worrying about the sad state in which international affairs find themselves. The Court of St. James is located in London, where the winters are long and dreary, and the fog and dampness soak into the bones of those who suffer from arthritis. Mandy and you will have to attend the social functions of the royal court at Buckingham Palace, where Mandy will have to bend her arthritic knees curtsying to the Queen, and you'll have to expose your arthritic knees to the gaze of all present by wearing knee breeches. After Mandy and you have considered all these drawbacks, let me know whether you still want me to go to the White House and ask President Eisenhower to give you the job of ambassador to the Court of St. James."

On his receipt of Senator Cooper's reply, George wrote the senator as follows: "Dear John Sherman, as always you're right. The job of ambassador to the Court of St. James wouldn't suit Mandy and me at all. I'll settle for the postmastership at Sleepy Hollow."

Chub Seawell was the Republican candidate for governor of North Carolina in 1952, when Dwight D. Eisenhower ran for president the first time. He generally approved of Eisenhower's policies. On one occasion, however, he was not altogether pleased with one of them, and he uttered this mild criticism: "President Eisenhower reminds me of the man who puts vitamins in his liquor to build himself up while he's tearing himself down."

Bill Lawrence, the American Broadcasting Company's television commentator, covered Senator Hubert H. Humphrey in his contest with Jack Kennedy in the West Virginia primary in 1960 for the delegates to the Democratic presidential convention. Lawrence telecast this information: "Hubert Humphrey is the only politician in America who has more solutions than the nation has problems."

After President Lyndon Johnson had initiated his Great Society, Hubert displayed his prowess as a problem solver when he spoke to the North Carolina Farmers Council at Raleigh. A member of the council said he was too old for Headstart and too young for Medicare and did not know what slot he fitted in the Great Society. Hubert immediately declared, "There's a meritorious spot for all good men like you in the Great Society. The Great Society is going to be right expensive. I'll appoint you a taxpayer of the Great Society."

Hubert Humphrey became one of the most beloved senators. Although he fought hard for the causes he cherished, he invariably manifested tolerance for those who disagreed with him.

❧ Thad Eure has served with highest efficiency as North Carolina's secretary of state since 1936. He captures political audiences with amusing anecdotes.

During the campaign of 1964 the Republican Party virtually monopolized roadside billboards in North Carolina and covered them with the picture of Barry Goldwater, their presidential candidate, and his slogan "In your heart you know he's right."

Thad Eure captivated the crowd at a Democratic rally in Wentworth, North Carolina, with this story. On his way to the rally, he said, he passed a roadside billboard, which, with the help of rain and wind, revealed the truth about the handsome Republican presidential candidate. The Republican political advertisement had been pasted over a display extolling the virtues of the Jones Company's meat products. The rain and wind had removed a part of the Republican advertisement and exposed a part of that underneath. As a consequence, one side of the billboard revealed the picture of the handsome Republican candidate and the slogan "In your heart you know he's right," and the other side revealed the truth respecting them—"Bologna."

❧ Except for Jack Kennedy and Lyndon Johnson, those who occupied the White House in my Senate years were rather dour.

President Kennedy had a subtle sense of humor, which he employed to disarm reporters who asked him pertinent and impertinent questions at presidential news conferences. An obviously hostile reporter asked him if his wealthy father, Joseph P. Kennedy, had not purchased the presidency for him. As I recall it, President Kennedy's reply was, "You don't know my father. He's a niggardly man. He told me not to buy a single vote that wasn't necessary."

While he had served with demonstrated ability as general counsel to the Senate Subcommittee on Permanent Investigations before his appointment as attorney general, Robert F. Kennedy had had no experience in the rough-and-tumble practice of law in the courtroom.

Another obviously hostile reporter asked President Kennedy at a news conference how he could justify appointing his legally inexperienced brother to the office of attorney general. The President replied, "I thought it would be good for Bobby to serve as attorney general a while before he begins to practice law."

❧ President Johnson's humor was of the anecdotal variety. Some of his favorite stories were too robust for inclusion in Sunday School literature. I will narrate one of his stories of a different kind, which emphasizes the importance of defending the decisions of the judiciary against unjust criticism.

A husband was in court for committing an assault and battery on his wife. After threatening to send him to jail, the judge relented, and suspended a jail term on condition he refrained from violence against his wife in the future.

On the following day the husband was before the same judge on the same charge. The judge said, "I'm going to send you to jail this time. The length of your sentence will depend on what excuse you can offer for your outrageous conduct."

Goaded by the judge's statement, the husband presented this explanation: "When I was before Your Honor yesterday, I suffered much tension. After Your Honor released me, my tension continued. To obtain relief from it, I stopped at several places on my way home and drank about a dozen mugs of beer. On my arrival home, my wife met me at the front steps, and called me a 'drunken bum.' Your Honor, her remark hurt my feelings. I realized, however, that I had drunk the beer on my way home, and she might have thought her remark justified. I held my temper, and didn't say a mumbling word in reply. Then she called me 'a trifling loafer.' That hurt my feelings. But I realized that I hadn't been able to find a job for six months, and thought that my wife may have believed I was a trifling loafer. So I held my temper, Your Honor, and never said a mumbling word in reply. But then, Your Honor, she said something I couldn't endure.

She said, 'If that damned judge who tried you this morning had had any sense, you would have been behind prison bars at this moment.' Your Honor, I couldn't bear to hear our fine judiciary being slandered like that. So I smacked her with my fist."

❦ Mendel Rivers, representative from the historic Charleston, South Carolina, district, was chairman of the House Armed Services Committee. He was noted for his wit and his power to secure military and naval projects for his district. He never had any trouble being reelected to the House because his constituents agreed that there was undeniable truth in his perennial slogan "Rivers delivers."

The Charleston Hibernian Society had been established in early days by Irish Catholics. As the decades passed, its membership became equally divided between Southern Catholics and Southern Protestants.

Some years ago I was invited to address the society at its annual banquet on the evening of Saint Patrick's Day, and Mendel was scheduled to introduce me. When he arose to perform this task, Mendel said, "Perhaps I should introduce myself before I present the speaker. I am Mendel O'Rivers of South Killarney."

My speech was well received. I began it with the aphorism of Father Abram Joseph Ryan, the poet laureate of the Confederacy, to the effect that a land without ruins is a land without memories, and a land without memories is a land without history. My theme was that history revealed Ireland and the South to be comparable lands which had suffered wrongs in times past at the hands of absent and distant rulers.

❦ While W. C. Fields, the gifted comedian, epitomized horse sense as the good judgment that keeps horses from betting on people, I equate horse sense with common sense. I displayed it when I visited Surry County, North Carolina, in a quest for reelection to the Senate.

To bolster my candidacy, Judge Franklin Freeman, of Dobson, took me to a horse show, where many people had gathered to watch the beautiful horses which were being exhibited and put through various capers. During a lull in these proceedings, Frank presented me to those in attendance with a generous introduction and assured them I was going to make a short speech which would not interfere with the show.

I thanked Frank for his introduction, expressed my pleasure in sharing with the audience the pleasant occasion, and assured its members I had no intention of making a speech by saying, "A politician who is fool enough to make a political speech at a horse show hasn't got any horse sense."

The audience disclosed its approval of my decision by vociferous applause. I am confident my silence won me more votes than anything I could have said would have done.

❧ The Raleigh bomb scare may merit remembrance. During the off-year election of 1970, Vice-President Spiro T. Agnew visited Raleigh to extol the Nixon administration and urge the voters of the Raleigh congressional district to support the Republican candidate for Congress rather than the Democratic incumbent, Nick Galifianakis.

Agnew and Nick were Americans of Greek ancestry. Nick was a colorful campaigner. When a constituent told Nick he had difficulty spelling Nick's surname, Nick responded, "Don't let that trouble you; I couldn't spell it myself until I was in the ninth grade." When another constituent told Nick he had difficulty pronouncing Nick's surname, Nick said, "It's easy if you'll remember it starts with a gal and ends with a kiss."

At the time it was announced that Agnew was going to campaign in Raleigh, the State Bureau of Investigation (SBI) and Raleigh police received many warnings that there would be dangerous bombings in Raleigh when Agnew came. Although I deemed these warnings to be hoaxes begotten by pranksters attending the colleges in the area, the SBI and the police deemed them to be serious and augmented their forces for the days of Agnew's visit with a bomb-demolition squad from Fort Bragg.

At the time I was traveling from one Democratic rally to another in North Carolina with my energetic aide, Rufus L. Edmisten, as my chauffeur. At the request of Larry O'Brien, chairman of the Democratic National Committee, and Nick Galifianakis, I went to Raleigh to help the Democrats counter Agnew's attacks on the party and Nick.

The Democrats planned a big rally in Fayetteville Street near the state capitol. They roped the street off to prevent vehicular traffic during the rally and erected a temporary speaker's platform in the middle of the street.

Rufus and I rode to the neighborhood of the platform just prior to the rally in an enclosed van which Nick used in campaigning. The van was parked with its doors securely locked, and Nick, Rufus, and I walked to the speaker's platform.

After the rally, which was quite spirited, Nick, Rufus, and I returned to the spot where we had left the parked van and discovered, to our consternation, that it had disappeared. We soon learned from hearsay, however, what had occurred during the rally.

The mother of another aide, Lacy Presnell, was highly skilled in the culinary art. She had cooked a large batch of cookies for Rufus and me, placed them in a big box wrapped in brown paper, and dispatched them to Nick's van by a courier, who was instructed to put them in the van. On finding the doors of the van locked, the courier left the brown package in a rack on top of the van.

Shortly thereafter the SBI and the police discovered the brown package and immediately decided that it contained a highly explosive bomb of deadly power.

Summoning the assistance of the squad from Fort Bragg, they drove the van with profound caution to an open field well outside Raleigh. When the geiger counter failed to indicate any bomb within the brown package, all of the members of the SBI, the police, and the bomb squad from Fort Bragg except the most valorous of them took shelter, and the most valorous of them hurled the brown package as far away as he could to determine whether it would explode when it hit the ground. It did not explode. Thereupon, they opened the package and discovered that it contained a large box full of cookie crumbs. On the advice of the SBI the box of cookie crumbs was taken to the State Crime Laboratory, which tested them to determine whether they harbored any explosive matter.

On learning of these events, Rufus and I called the SBI by phone, and demanded the return of our cookies. The SBI rejected our demand, justifying its action by explaining that the cookies had been reduced to crumbs and the crumbs were not palatable because the State Crime Laboratory had impregnated them with a noxious substance in testing them for explosive ingredients.

No bombs were heard in Raleigh during Agnew's visit except the verbal bombs exploded by him and me.

❧ I have enshrined Leon Jaworski, of Texas, among my heroes because of his service to the American bar as one of its outstanding leaders and to our country as special prosecutor in the Watergate tragedy. After the news media announced that he was forming a nationwide committee of Democrats for Ronald Reagan, he contacted me by long-distance telephone and extended me an invitation to become one of the members of the committee.

I declined his invitation. I told him that I had invariably supported all Democratic presidential nominees since I had cast my first vote for Governor James M. Cox, of Ohio, in 1920, and that I was going to be numbered among Jimmy Carter's supporters in his bid for reelection in 1980.

"I'm bound to confess," I went on, "that President Carter has instilled some foreboding in respect to the outcome of the election in my Democratic heart by the televised campaign sermon he preached to the black congregation in Ebenezer Baptist Church in Atlanta a few evenings ago. As I interpret his campaign sermon, President Carter said states' rights had become as obscene as any four-letter word, and Ronald Reagan had proved his unfitness for the presidency by telling a Mississippi audience in a recent speech that he believed in states' rights. While Jimmy Carter is going to get my vote, I fear that his campaign sermon may have lost him the absentee votes of my three granduncles and their Confederate comrades who died in the Civil War fighting with General Robert E. Lee for states' rights."

My fear materialized. Jimmy Carter lost the electoral votes of all Southern states except Georgia.

Chapter 6

Humor in Religion

ও ও ও

I possess the right to tell humorous stories about Presbyterians because I give them my religious allegiance. I inherited the right to talk about Episcopalians from my mother, who was reared in their church. I acquired the right to joke about the Methodists by practicing their doctrine of falling from grace.

I claim the right to laugh about the Baptists on the basis of an assertion made by my old friend Gordon Bush, commander of the American Legion Post in Lenoir, North Carolina, some years ago. In introducing my collegemate at Chapel Hill James T. Pritchett, of the Lenoir bar, as the keynote speaker at an Armistice Day banquet, Gordon stated, "Jim Pritchett is an elder in the Presbyterian church. For fear some of you may not know what a Presbyterian is, I'll explain. A Presbyterian is a shallow-water Baptist."

Incidentally, Lenoir has always been a repository of religious truth. Dr. Gus McLean, the beloved pastor of its First Presbyterian Church, remonstrated with his young son for fighting a public school classmate who was Jewish. He said, "Son, you ought to be ashamed of yourself. Don't you know that Jesus was a Jew?" "Father, I'm sorry," his son replied. "I know God is a Presbyterian, but I had no idea that Jesus was a Jew."

Honesty compels me to confess that I have simply usurped the privilege of recounting Catholic stories. My favorite story in this category was told to me by a Catholic friend.

A young priest who had just completed his studies at the seminary was enthusiastic with his first parish assignment. He visited the bishop of the diocese and said, "Bishop, I think our Church ought to utilize innovations. We have drive-in banks, drive-in theaters, drive-in restaurants, and the like. I think we ought to establish a drive-in confessional and make it possible for those who find it inconvenient to visit a church for this purpose to drive in, make their confessions, and go on their way."

The bishop told the young priest he had grave misgivings concerning his proposal. The young priest was persuasively eloquent, however, and the bishop authorized him to establish a drive-in confessional on an experimental basis.

The young priest did so. After a time, the bishop sent for him and told him that he had had many complaints from the faithful concerning the project and that he would have to close the drive-in confessional.

The young priest protested, "But, Bishop, you gave me permission to establish it."

The bishop replied, "I gave you permission to do so upon a purely experimental basis. I didn't give you permission, however, to install the glaring neon signs overhead saying, 'Toot and tell, or go to hell.'"

❦   In 1965 my wife and I visited Rome and had an audience with Pope Paul VI, who impressed us with his profound piety, wisdom, and humility. The pope gave a beautiful rosary to my wife and a medal commemorating the recently held Ecumenical Conference to me.

My wife has a most unselfish and understanding heart. She said, "As a Presbyterian, I cannot use this beautiful rosary in religious worship. Although I am strongly tempted to keep it as a precious gift from the pope, I am going to give it to the wife of Colonel Mozingo, our military escort, who is a devout Catholic. I know she will prize it." And that is what my wife did.

After we had seen the pope, an American journalist interviewed me. In so doing, he expressed the hope that my impression of the pope was as complimentary as that of the congressman who had had an audience with the pope sometime before. Upon being asked what he thought of the pope, the congressman replied, "He seems to be sort of a religious fellow."

❧ In days of yore, a few Baptist clergymen in North Carolina tended to overemphasize baptism by immersion as the most acceptable route to salvation. One old Baptist minister preached every Sunday on baptism by immersion. His exclusive preoccupation with this theological doctrine wearied his congregation, and some of its members begged the deacons to find some way to give them surcease.

The deacons, who did not wish to offend the sensibilities of their old pastor, undertook to solve the problem by diplomatic means. They informed him that they wanted to test his ability to preach extemporaneously, and that to this end they wanted him to refrain from preparing a sermon for the following Sunday and to preach on that day on a text which they would present to him at the time for the sermon.

The deacons searched the Scriptures for a text which was unrelated to baptism by immersion. They selected the opening verse of Genesis: "In the beginning, God created the heaven and the earth."

When they handed the text to him, the old preacher read it aloud three times, and announced to the congregation, "If I remember geography aright, the earth is one-fourth land and three-fourths water. This brings me to my subject: Baptism by immersion."

❧ In bygone days, some Baptist ministers immersed converts during warm weather in the waters of nearby creeks. One Tar Heel, whom I shall call John, was an incorrigible poker player. For years he resisted the importunings of his wife, a devout Baptist, who deemed gambling a cardinal sin, to forgo his favorite pastime.

Their son, Little Willie, had decided to join the Baptist church and be baptized in the creek. His mother begged John to repent of his evil habit and join the church and be baptized with Little Willie. John reluctantly agreed and promised his wife that he would never have anything more to do with cards.

At the appointed time, the preacher led Little Willie into the creek, and baptized him. After Little Willie had taken his place beside his mother on the creek bank, the preacher led John into the creek and immersed him.

As John was baptized, the following cards emerged from his hip pocket and floated face up on the water: the ace of spades, the king of spades, the queen of spades, the jack of spades, and the ten of spades.

When John's wife saw this unholy sight, she exclaimed, "Look there, Little Willie. Your Pa's lost, your Pa's lost."

Little Willie responded, "Ma, if Pa loses with a hand like that, he ought to go to hell."

❧ Sometimes people acquire membership in churches whose dogmas and usages are inconsistent with their thoughts and deeds. Zeb Vance had a brother, Robert Brank Vance, who represented North Carolina's western-most congressional district in Congress after valiant service as a brigadier general of the Confederacy.

Zeb said, "Brother Bob and I got mixed up when we selected our respective churches. Bob is a Methodist. He believes in falling from grace, but never falls. I'm a Presbyterian. I don't believe in falling from grace, but I'm always falling."

❧ The drunk who staggered into the rear of Grace Episcopal Church in my hometown, Morganton, one Sunday morning was certain he had found the right church. At the time the congregation was reciting this passage of the General Confession from the Book of Common Prayer: "We have left undone the things which we ought to have done, and we have done the things which we ought not to have done." When the members of the congregation concluded the general confession, the drunk said to himself, "At long last I've found a church after my own heart."

❧ My maternal grandmother's colorful cousin Wistar Tate was sure he had joined the right church when he united with the Episcopal church in his twilight years. According to rumors which still survive, Cousin Wistar was an erring sinner who often forsook the straight-and-narrow path for ways he found more appealing.

After he joined the Episcopal church, a friend congratulated him on finally exhibiting enough wisdom to unite with a religious body. His friend stated further that he was somewhat surprised by Wistar's choice because so many of his relatives were Presbyterians.

Cousin Wistar explained, "I thought it was time for me to join a church. Before I did so, however, I studied the creeds and practices of all the churches in Morganton and decided that the Episcopal church is the church for me. There are only two ways to get out of the Episcopal church after you're received as a member. One is to die, and the other is to get religion. I can assure you I'm now a full-fledged life member."

🐿 Lieutenant Governor Will Newland was a staunch Methodist. His wife was a devout Presbyterian. The Methodists of Lenoir were erecting a new house of worship. As the projected cost of the edifice had been grossly underestimated, they were always calling on Governor Newland for contributions, and Governor Newland was answering the calls with his accustomed generosity. Finally, Mrs. Newland suggested that the governor was giving too much of his financial resources to a single cause. He thereupon assured his wife that the Methodists would not ask him for another contribution. When Mrs. Newland asked him how he knew this, he replied, "I told the Methodists this morning that if they asked me for another penny, I'd transfer my membership to your church, and go to hell with the Presbyterians."

🐿 Our oldest grandson, Jimmy Ervin, who was at the time the only grandchild my wife and I had, was accustomed to visit us on Sundays and dine with us during his early years.

I digress to note that our son, the chairman of the Burke County Democrats at the time, had indoctrinated Jimmy with the faith once delivered to the Democratic saints.

One Sunday a neighbor visited us. He asked Jimmy if he had been to Sunday School that morning. Jimmy said, "Yes, I went to the Presbyterian Sunday School."

The neighbor asked him, "Jimmy, are you a Presbyterian?"

Jimmy responded, "Oh, no. I'm not a Presbyterian. I'm a Democrat."

🐿 An amusing story, whose origin is unknown to me, concerns a young Southern Presbyterian minister who was serving in his first pastorate. His salary was low, and he was having difficulty keeping his financial buckle and tongue together. His young wife brought home a beautiful, but expensive, dress which she had bought on his credit at a neighborhood store. He remonstrated with her, "Dear, you ought to have remembered the state of my finances, and refrained from buying that dress." She explained, "I entered the store with the expectation of buying some inexpensive handkerchiefs. The proprietor persuaded me to try on the dress, and view myself in the mirror wearing the dress. It was so beautiful I could not resist the temptation to buy it."

The young preacher said, "You should have remembered the Scriptures, and told the devil, 'Get thee behind me Satan.' "

"I did," the young wife responded. "But it didn't do any good. As soon as he got behind me, the devil whispered in my ear, 'The dress fits as nicely and looks as beautiful in the back as it does in the front.' "

❦   Joseph B. Clower, Jr., my pastor in Morganton, delivered lectures to his congregation on the differences in the doctrines of various denominations. In distinguishing between the Presbyterian and Methodist churches, he declared, "The Presbyterian church is Calvinistic. It believes in predestination, i.e., that everything which is going to happen was planned by the Almighty at the beginning of time, and that mankind cannot alter the divine plan. The Methodist church, on the contrary, adheres to Arminian doctrines and rejects predestination. By this I mean, the Methodists believe that when anything happens, the Almighty is just as surprised as anybody else."

❦   All people would embrace Presbyterianism if they fully comprehended the doctrine of predestination. Although I cannot explain it in theological terms, I can make its real significance plain by relating a story, which may be apocryphal, about Major Robert Lewis Dabney, the Presbyterian minister who served as chief chaplain to Stonewall Jackson's command.

I cannot forbear digressing to recount the accolade that Robert E. Lee bestowed on his valiant lieutenant Stonewall Jackson. After Jackson's left arm had been amputated on account of wounds suffered at Chancellorsville and he lay dying in the cottage near Bowling Green, Virginia, Lee sent Jackson this message: "You have lost your left arm, but I have lost my right."

According to the story, Major Dabney always preached to Jackson's men on predestination. He assured them that the Almighty had planned and predestined everything which was ever going to happen. Consequently, he further assured them, if they were predestined to be killed or wounded by a Yankee bullet, they could not possibly escape the bullet; on the contrary, if they were not predestined to be killed or wounded by a Yankee bullet, no Yankee bullet could harm them. He added that for these reasons they ought to maintain absolute serenity in the midst of the hottest battle.

One day a skirmish occurred while Major Dabney was visiting the front. As the Yankee bullets began to kick up dust spots around him, the major ran as fast as he could and jumped behind a big tree.

A Confederate private, who had already taken refuge behind the tree, remarked, "Major Dabney, you don't practice what you preach."

The major inquired, "What do you mean, my good man?"

The Confederate soldier replied, "You're always telling us that everything that's going to happen has been planned and predestined by the Almighty; that we can't possibly escape our predestined fate; and that for this reason we should always be calm in battle. I noticed, however, that when the Yankee bullets began to kick up dust spots around you, you forgot about predestination, resorted to free will, undertook to save yourself, and ran and jumped behind this tree."

Major Dabney explained, "My good man, you do not fully understand the doctrine of predestination. You overlook two significant factors. The tree was predestined to be here, and I was predestined to run and jump behind it."

❦   Dr. Robert Laban Abernethy had one weakness which is not characteristic of the clergy. He always dressed himself at the height of the fashion of the day by wearing a high silk hat and a long swallowtail coat and carrying a gold-headed walking cane.

He happened to go to Marion, North Carolina, to attend some church function on the day the Democrats were holding a convention there to nominate a candidate for Congress. All persons seeking political offices in all the nearby counties had joined the delegates and swelled the ranks of those who had come to Marion for the convention.

As Dr. Abernethy was walking to the church meeting, a somewhat inebriated delegate observed him arrayed in his habiliments of glory and surmised that he must be a candidate for one of the highest offices within the gift of the people.

The delegate slapped Dr. Abernethy on the back and asked, "Brother, what is the office for which you are a candidate?" Dr. Abernethy, who was a man of great dignity, drew himself up to his full height and replied, "My friend, I am a candidate for the Kingdom of Heaven." The delegate assured him, "Brother, you're sure to get elected. Nobody else at this convention is running for that place."

❦ Karlton Giles, who was known as Kalt, and Uncle Billy Hallyburton were boyhood friends. They swam, fished, and hunted together. As young men, they attended a Methodist revival and joined that church at the same time. They made mutual pledges to pray for each other as long as they lived. Each of them was an ardent Democrat.

Uncle Billy made his home in Morganton. Kalt Giles resided in Glen Alpine, six miles to the west. The Populists made their appearance as a political party in the 1890s. They had panaceas for all the nation's ills.

Uncle Billy attended a Populist meeting. The speaker was most lavish in assuring his audience that if they were entrusted with political power, the Populists would speedily convert America into Utopia.

Uncle Billy was impulsive at times. He arose and declared that he was going to abandon the Democrats and support the Populists in the forthcoming election.

Shortly after the following midnight, Uncle Billy was awakened by someone banging on his door. He called out, "Who's that banging on my door at this ungodly hour?" "It's me, Kalt Giles," the visitor responded.

Uncle Billy inquired, "What's troubling you, Kalt?" Kalt replied, "Brother Billy, I heard a foul slander about you just before midnight, and I hitched up my horse and buggy and drove to Morganton to hear you deny it with your own lips."

Uncle Billy asked, "Brother Kalt, what was the foul slander you heard about me?" Kalt answered, "I heard you had left the Democrats and jined the Populists." "That is no slander," Uncle Billy said. "That's the truth."

Kalt thereupon delivered this ultimatum to Uncle Billy: "Many years ago we joined the Methodist church together and promised to pray for each other as long as we lived. I have been faithful to that promise. Every night before closing my eyes in sleep, I've gotten down on my knees and remembered you in my supplications to the Almighty. But since you've left the Democrats and jined the Populists, Brother Billy, I'm going to let you do your own damned praying hereafter."

❧   Kalt Giles's partisanship was not restricted to politics. As a consequence, he was in demand as a character witness in judicial proceedings. He testified for the accused in a criminal case and deposed that all his witnesses were persons of high character and that all the witnesses for the prosecution, except his close kinsman Butler Giles, were persons of low repute.

Counsel for the defense refrained from making an inquiry of Kalt concerning the reputation of Butler, who had testified for the prosecution and who was one of Burke County's finest citizens. The prosecuting attorney noted this omission and insisted that Kalt tell the jury about the reputation of his kinsman.

Kalt did not want to say anything hurtful to the defense or helpful to the prosecution. Moreover, he did not desire to say anything derogatory about his kinsman. After discovering he could not evade the prosecuting attorney's questions by feigning deafness, Kalt admitted that he knew Butler's reputation. He added, "He is just one of us Gileses. His reputation is tolerable."

❧   Bill Banner's home and gristmill stood on the bank of the river near Banner Elk in Avery County. The rains descended, the river rose, and the flood waters threatened to wash the home and gristmill away.

Mrs. Banner said, "Nothing can save our home and your gristmill except a miracle or prayer. There's no miracle in sight. You had better get down on your knees and ask the Good Lord to save our home and your gristmill."

Bill obeyed. Unaccustomed as he was to praying, he fell to his knees and made this moving supplication to the Almighty: "O, Lord, I'm Bill Banner. I've got a home and a gristmill at the river near Banner Elk, North Carolina. The flood is about to wash them away. I'm not always ding-donging in your ears asking you for something like Preacher Tufts is. But I'm compelled to ask you for a favor now. Please spare my home and mill. If you'll do that, I will seldom, if ever, ask you for another favor as long as I live. Yours truly, Bill Banner."

❦   Like Mrs. Banner, Will Rainey, of Burke County, had faith in the power of prayer. Will was on a protracted drunk. He felt bad, and feared he was dying. He importuned his wife to pray for him. His wife prayed, "O, Lord, have mercy on my poor drunk husband." Will interjected, "Don't tell the Lord I'm drunk. Tell him I'm sick."

❦   Because of his gift as a raconteur, Doggie Hatcher, my old National Guard comrade, always provoked his audience to laughter with this story.

An impoverished church in the boondocks had worn out its old hymn books by long use, and was experiencing difficulty in its efforts to raise contributions sufficient to replace them. The enterprising agent of an enterprising manufacturer of medicines offered to have his employer print new hymnals and donate them to the church if the church was willing for them to include some limited advertisements of the manufacturer's wares.

The church accepted the offer, and the agent delivered the newly printed hymnals to the church a few minutes after the church's Christmas service had begun. Although he had no opportunity to examine the contents of the new hymnals, the pastor distributed them among the members of the congregation and announced, "The congregation will stand and sing our favorite Christmas song, hymn 57, 'Hark the Herald Angels Sing.'"

The members of the congregation arose, opened their new hymnals, and discovered that the first verse of hymn 57 had been revised to read:

Hark, the herald angels sing,
Smith's pills are just the thing; ·
Peace on earth and mercy mild,
Two for man, and one for child.

🦌 I am indebted to United States District Judge Richard C. Erwin
for this story. George, who had lived a riotous life on earth, made a
deathbed repentance and got through the pearly gates by the skin of
his teeth. After some time in heaven, George went to Saint Peter
and said, "I'm not happy in heaven. The golden streets are hard on
my feet. I'm tired of hearing the angels twanging on their harps.
Won't you let me go to hell a little while and visit my old friends?"

Saint Peter replied, "Your request is highly irregular. But I don't
want anybody in heaven to be unhappy. I'll let you visit your friends
in hell, provided you return to heaven by six o'clock sharp."

By Saint Peter's grace, George visited his old friends in hell and
had such a joyous time with them he forgot the deadline. He didn't
return to heaven until nine o'clock—three hours late. Saint Peter
chastised him verbally and declared that he would be compelled to
discipline George severely for ignoring the deadline.

George said, "Saint Peter, you won't have to do that. I didn't come
to stay. I just came to get my clothes."

🦌 During our sojourn in Washington, my wife and I attended the
New York Avenue Presbyterian Church and heard its famous Scottish pastor, Peter Marshall, preach. Another Scot, the Right Reverend James Cleland, dean of the beautiful chapel at Duke University,
asked me whether I shared the view that Peter Marshall was the
most profound preacher in America. I replied, "I really don't know.
I've always been entranced by Peter Marshall's Scottish brogue and
have never analyzed what he says." Dean Cleland noted, "Scots
have an advantage over other clergymen. When we turn on our
brogue, our hearers are intrigued by it, and assume we are preach-
ing with profundity, no matter how inane what we say may be."

🦌 On the evening of Armistice Day many years ago I had the
privilege of being the guest speaker at an American Legion post in

Charlotte. The post commander told this story relating to Father Best, a Catholic priest, who was the post chaplain.

As a passenger on a city bus, Father Best was reading the *Charlotte News*. He was nevertheless somewhat irritated by a vociferous drunk seated on the opposite side of the aisle who puffed on a cheap cigar and ogled the girls as they entered or left the bus.

Without so much as a "by-your-leave," the drunk suddenly reached across the aisle, grabbed Father Best's newspaper, and proceeded to read it for several moments.

By this time, Father Best was completely exasperated by the drunk.

Suddenly the drunk looked at Father Best and inquired: "What causes neuralgia?" Father Best replied, "There are many causes. If you get drunk on mean liquor, blow evil-smelling cigar smoke into the faces of other people, and ogle the girls, you are certain to get it."

The drunk said, "Thank you, sir. Thank you, sir. I was just wondering. Your paper says that Bishop Sheen is suffering from neuralgia."

❧   I have related in jesting guise some humorous stories which had their origin in the sacred realm of religion. Before ending this phase of my remarks on humor, I wish to say that it is impossible to overmagnify the strength and comfort that religion gives to men and women. The most beautiful of all prayers is enshrined in the Book of Common Prayer of the Protestant Episcopal church.

> O Lord, support us all the day long, until the shadows lengthen and the evening comes, and the busy world is hushed, and the fever of life is over, and our work is done. Then in thy mercy grant us a safe lodging, and a holy rest, and peace at the last. Amen.

I entertain this abiding conviction: Religious faith is the most potent force in the universe. It affords us the surest guidance for our perplexing days in this troublous world and gives us the hope of a blessed immortality in the world to come.

Religious faith is not a storm cellar to which men and women can flee for refuge from the storms of life. It is, instead, an inner spiritual strength which enables them to face those storms with hope and serenity. Religious faith has the miraculous power to lift ordinary human beings to greatness in seasons of stress. Religious faith is to be found in the promises of God.

At a time when her physical eyesight was failing, Annie Johnson Flint saw these promises with the eyes of faith and revealed them to us with rare beauty in her poem "What God Hath Promised."

> God hath not promised
> Skies always blue,
> Flower-strewn pathways
> All our lives through;
> God hath not promised
> Sun without rain,
> Joy without sorrow,
> Peace without pain.
>
> But God hath promised
> Strength for the day,
> Rest for the labor,
> Light for the way,
> Grace for the trials,
> Help from above,
> Unfailing sympathy,
> Undying love.

Chapter 7

Humor in
the Law

❧ ❧ ❧

I was admitted to the North Carolina bar in 1919 and graduated from Harvard Law School in 1922. With the exception of the time I spent on the bench and in legislative bodies, I have devoted my major energies ever since to the practice of law. My judicial experience embraced two years as judge of the Burke County Criminal Court, seven years as a North Carolina superior court judge, and six years as a North Carolina Supreme Court justice.

I entertain the abiding convictions that the administration of justice is government's most sacred obligation; that government cannot confer on a citizen a more exalted responsibility than that of judge; that this responsibility is reflected in Edmund Burke's phrase "the cold neutrality of the impartial judge"; and that his contemporaries bestow on a judge the highest encomium when they adjudge him to be a just and upright judge.

The most trying task of the judge of a sensitive heart is that of presiding in criminal trials in which he must execute justice in mercy without being forgetful of the truth that society and the victims of crime are just as much entitled to justice as the accused.

Walter Malone, the judge and poet of Memphis, Tennessee, knew something of the heartaches of such a judge, and enshrined them for us in the poem entitled "To A Judge."

> O thou who wieldest for one fleeting day
> The power that belongs alone to God:
> O idol moulded out of common clay,
> To sway one little hour an iron rod,
>
> Dost thou not tremble to assume thy seat,

And judge thy fellow-travelers to the tomb?
Dost thou not falter as thy lips repeat
Thy Comrade's downfall, thy Companion's doom?

A word from you, and Fortune flies away,
While silks and satins tatters into rags;
The banquet revellers scatter in dismay,
And Pride and Pomp haul down their flaunting flags.

You sentence, and your brother, lost to light,
Sits crouching in a dungeon dark and damp;
No stream can ever wash his brow to white
From inky impress of your iron stamp.

He bids farewell to all things fair and sweet,
Exiled from fields and forests, blooms and birds;
He hears no more his children's pattering feet,
Their liquid lisping of their mother's words.

Your hapless fellow-man must heed your call
To mount the scaffold, you have power to kill,
And Life, the greatest miracle of all,
Is ended in obedience to your will.

Your softest speech may smirch the fairest name,
What reputations hang upon your breath!
Your fiats may translate from fame to shame,
Or bring dishonor blacker-hued than death.

Then be so wise, so merciful, so kind,
The words "Well done!" may never come begrudged;
For thou, the master, shalt a Master find,
And thou who judgest soon shalt be adjudged.

A judge of sensitive heart could not long survive these heartaches if it were not for the humor that occasionally lightens his burdens.

❧ James M. Leach, Confederate soldier and official and eminent lawyer of Lexington, North Carolina, regaled his friends with this story, whose authenticity I cannot affirm.

Jim Leach had a client who was scheduled to be tried in the superior court of Rowan County on an indictment charging him with stealing a watch. He registered as a guest at the old Mount Vernon Hotel in the late afternoon of the Sunday before the court was to be convened and discovered that the judge who was to preside was also registered there. Before dinner he and the judge repaired to the hotel bar, which was open for business even on the Sabbath, to whet their appetites. At his request the bartender mixed several ingredients in the judge's drinks, and the judge lapsed into a state of unconsciousness after taking his seat at a dining room table. Jim crammed the judge's pockets full of the knives, forks, and spoons, assisted him to his room, and left him on his bed fully clothed in an unconscious state. Being an honest man, the judge returned the cutlery to the dining room the following morning with the truthful explanation that he had no idea how they had come into his possession.

When the court reached Jim Leach's case the following day, the prosecutor called two witnesses to the stand to testify against his client. The first witness, a jeweler, deposed that late one afternoon Jim's client came to his shop and asked to see a watch; that he placed several watches before him and turned his back on Jim's client to wait on another customer; that on looking around he discovered that Jim's client was gone and so was his best watch; that he procured a search warrant authorizing a search of the person and premises of Jim's client and gave it to the sheriff; and that shortly thereafter the sheriff returned the lost watch to him. The sheriff testified that, acting under the search warrant, he searched the accused's home and person and found the watch in his pocket.

After the prosecutor rested his case, Jim called his client to the stand. His client testified that he had no recollection of visiting the jeweler's shop or seeing the watch until the sheriff came to his home and discovered it in his pocket. On being directed by Jim to disclose what he did on the day named in the indictment, the client said, "I had worked hard all day. Feeling the need of a stimulant, I went to the bar of the Mount Vernon Hotel and had a few drinks. That's all I knew until the sheriff came to my home, waked me up, and found the watch in my pocket."

The judge roused himself from his judicial lethargy and asked Jim's client, "Where did you say you had a few drinks?" "At the bar of the Mount Vernon Hotel," he responded. The judge said, "The liquor they serve there will make anybody steal. Mr. Clerk, enter a verdict of not guilty."

❧ Jeff Curtis bought a jug of liquor at a Morganton saloon and walked westward on the Southern Railway tracks on his way home. While en route he was struck and injured by a Southern train. He retained the beloved John Marion Mull, of the Morganton bar, to sue the railroad in his behalf for damages. John Mull, who subsequently became one of Burke County's most knowledgeable lawyers, was then a young lawyer without an understanding of the last-clear-chance doctrine. He filed a complaint in behalf of Jeff alleging, in substance, that at the time he was struck by the train Jeff was sitting on the end of a cross-tie.

Judge Alphonso C. Avery, of Morganton, who had served with distinction for some years on the North Carolina Supreme Court, was defeated for reelection in 1894, and returned to Morganton to practice law. Subsequent to his return, which occurred about eight months after the institution of Jeff's suit, Judge Avery was retained to assist Mull in the trial of the case.

Judge Avery quickly observed that, as the facts were stated in the complaint, the engineer could claim that he assumed that Jeff was in possession of his faculties and would step off the track in time to avoid injury. He filed an amended complaint which alleged that at the time he was stricken by the train Jeff was lying helpless and prostrate on the track and that the engineer could have avoided striking him if he had been keeping a reasonable lookout.

When the case was tried in Burke County Superior Court, Captain George Bason, a resourceful lawyer who was attorney for the railroad, cross-examined the plaintiff. After reading to Jeff portions of his original and amended complaints, Captain Bason put to Jeff this inquiry: "I ask you if John Mull did not seat you on the end of a cross-tie and leave you sitting there for eight months until Judge Avery stepped down from the Supreme Court and laid you helpless and prostrate on the track?" Jeff responded, "Yes sir, Captain Bason; that's the way it was."

❦   Job Hicks revered the word of the Lord. An acquaintance of his, John Watts, took a notion he had been called to preach the Gospel and adopted the practice of doing so in any little country church which would allow him to occupy its pulpit. While he was well versed in his profession as a brick mason, Watts was woefully ignorant in matters of theology.

One Sunday, Hicks imbibed a little too much Burke County corn liquor, a rather potent beverage. After so doing, he walked by a little country church, saw Watts in the pulpit, and heard him expounding to the congregation his peculiar version of a biblical text. Hicks entered the church, staggered to the pulpit, grabbed Watts by the collar, dragged him to the door, and threw him out of the church.

When the time came for the pronouncement of sentence on the jury's verdict of guilty, Judge William Smith O'Brien Robinson, the presiding judge, observed, "Mr. Hicks, when you were guilty of such unseemly conduct on the Sabbath Day, you must have been too drunk to realize what you were doing." Hicks responded, "It is true, Your Honor, that I had had several drinks, but I wouldn't want Your Honor to think I was so drunk that I could stand by and hear the word of the Lord being *mummicked* up like that without doing something about it."

❦   While he was representing Burke County in the North Carolina House of Representatives in 1907, Isaac T. Avery induced the General Assembly to enact a local law making it a crime for any person to bring into Burke County in any one day more than half a gallon of spirituous liquors. Shortly afterward, Robert B. Peebles, of distant Northampton County, who was one of the state's extraordinary superior court judges, was the presiding judge at Burke County Superior Court.

An accused pleaded guilty to the violation of Burke County's local law. Quite naturally, Judge Peebles was not familiar with this local law, and inquired of the lawyer for the accused as to the nature of his client's offense. On being advised of the provisions of the local law, Judge Peebles declared, "That law is clearly unconstitutional. I brought more than half a gallon of spirituous liquor into Burke County when I came to preside over this court." Judge Peebles then ordered the clerk to make this entry: "The plea of guilty is stricken out, the indictment is quashed, and the case is dismissed because the law is unconstitutional."

❧   James E. Boyd was the judge of the United States District Court for the Western District of North Carolina. His love for humor prompted him to kid virtually everyone who appeared in his courtroom. Joshua Hawkins sat in the back of the district courtroom at Statesville waiting for the district attorney to call for trial an indictment alleging that he had operated an illegal distillery on his farm in the South Mountains of Burke County.

The district attorney called out his name and he answered and walked into the bar to be tried. On ascertaining that the first name of the accused was Joshua, Judge Boyd inquired, "Mr. Hawkins, are you the Joshua the Bible tells us about who made the sun stand still at Jericho?" "No, Your Honor," Hawkins responded. "I'm the Joshua who's accused of making the moonshine in Burke."

❧   James M. Gudger, a famed trial lawyer and wit of Asheville, had an extensive practice throughout western North Carolina. He attended the superior court of Mitchell County at a time when the law authorized druggists to supply customers a limited quantity of liquor for medical purposes on the prescription of a physician.

Jim Gudger drafted a document in the form of a prescription for one pint of spirituous liquor, signed it "J. M. Gudger, M.D.," and sent it by an obliging courier to a drugstore in Bakersville. A cautious friend who had witnessed this transaction said, "Jim, you are treating the law with contempt in representing yourself to be a physician." In assuring his friend he was in error, Gudger said, "The words *J. M. Gudger, M.D.* don't mean that J. M. Gudger is a medical doctor; they mean that J. M. Gudger is mighty dry."

❧   I now forsake North Carolina to tell a Georgia story. An old lawyer in Blue Ridge, Georgia, was appalled by the thought that he might be buried in the earth after death. He employed an architect who specialized in that area to design for him a mausoleum, which he had erected in the town cemetery.

The old lawyer was known throughout the community as the Colonel. An old farmer visited him in his law office and said, "Colonel, I've been hearing a lot of talk about your mausoleum. So I went to the town cemetery this morning and inspected it. My long friendship for you compels me to tell you that you made a serious mistake when you built your mausoleum."

The Colonel, who was inordinately proud of his mausoleum, said, "That's ridiculous. My mausoleum was designed by the finest architect in that field in America."

"I don't care if it was designed by the finest architect in the universe," the old farmer rejoined. "It's defective in a most serious way."

The Colonel said, "Since you know so much about mausoleums, suppose you tell me what's wrong with it."

The old farmer said, "You forgot to install a fire escape."

ఌ   This story is theologically related to the tale of the enterprising Arnica Salve salesman which was current in my youth. Arnica Salve was a medical preparation that was regarded as a sure cure for all the external miseries of man.

A religious zealot had painted in massive letters on an enormous rock plainly visible from a nearby highway this inquiry: "What are you going to do in the next world?" As he passed by and observed the inquiry, the enterprising salesman painted this advice in massive letters under the inquiry: "Use Arnica Salve. It's good for burns."

ఌ   Risden Tyler Bennett, of Wadesboro, in Anson County, was one of North Carolina's most illustrious sons. After valorous service as a colonel in the Army of the Confederacy, he became a superior court judge. His stalwart frame and belligerent beard commanded respect and obedience.

He was presiding in the Wilkes County Superior Court. When a notorious desperado failed to appear in conformity to his bond to answer a multitude of accusations, Judge Bennett directed the clerk to issue an *instanter capias* for the arrest of the accused and ordered the sheriff to serve it on him without delay.

Someone in the courtroom stated that the accused was at the top of a stairway on the other side of the street and was threatening to kill anyone who undertook to arrest him.

The judge said, "Sheriff, do your duty." The sheriff begged off, saying, "Judge, I have a wife and six children dependent on me for support. The accused is a desperate character."

The judge said, "Sheriff, loan me your pistol."

The sheriff handed a pistol to the judge, who declared, "Court is recessed for fifteen minutes."

The judge walked across the street and saw the desperado armed with a pistol standing at the top of the stairway. The desperado threatened, "If you come nearer, I'll shoot you."

"You can't scare me," Judge Bennett nonchalantly replied. He then pointed the pistol at the accused's head and said, "I'll give you exactly thirty seconds to drop your pistol, walk down the steps, and surrender." Taken aback, the desperado did exactly that. Judge Bennett escorted him to the courthouse, had him lodged in jail to await trial, returned the pistol to the sheriff, and declared the court open for business without comment.

After distinguished service on the bench, Judge Bennett was elected to Congress from the Anson District. He soon announced he would not seek reelection and that anyone aspiring to succeed him could begin campaigning.

In explaining his decision to retire the judge said, "When our congressman comes to Anson County to speak on the Fourth of July, we always turn out in multitudes and pay homage to him. After I went to Washington, I discovered that congressmen are as common in Washington as hound dogs are in Anson County. I have no desire to stay in Congress."

In his twilight years, Judge Bennett habitually wrote poems eulogizing departed friends, and the local newspaper invariably published them. A literary critic declared that by his poetry Judge Bennett had added another terror to death.

In after years, government emulated him in adding its terrors to death by exacting inheritance taxes from taxpayers making their exits from this world.

❧ I am now going to tell two stories suggested to me by the captivating memoirs of Judge Arthur G. Powell, of Georgia, entitled *I Can Go Home Again*, and thereby violate my personally imposed limitation not to tell stories that appear in the books of others.

Since somebody has borrowed and neglected to return my copy of Judge Powell's memoirs, I will present his stories in conformity with my faulty recollection, rather than quote them.

A hard-shell preacher in southwest Georgia preached a sermon on hell. To emphasize its infinite heat, he said, "If the Almighty made one heap of all the fat lightwood [rich pine] in Georgia, set it afire, waited till it was burning at fever heat, multiplied that heat billions of times, and took a poor sinner out of the coolest spot in hell and dropped him into the midst of the fire, the change in temperature would be so great the poor sinner would freeze to death in less than a minute."

✻ Superior Court Judge David Roberts, of Georgia, rightly prided himself on his knowledge of the laws governing titles to land. Judge Roberts delivered his charge to the petit jury in a land suit tried by him in south Georgia with his customary care, and was exasperated by the subsequent ruling of the Supreme Court of Georgia granting the losing litigant a new trial on the ground he had committed legal error in his charge. The ruling was made pursuant to an opinion drafted for the court by Chief Justice William H. Fish. Judge Roberts asserted far and wide that the opinion must have been written by Clayton, the black messenger of the court, who had no education or erudition in law.

Thereafter Judge Roberts visited the office of the clerk of the Georgia Supreme Court. On learning this, Chief Justice Fish invited Judge Roberts into the court's conference room, where he and the other justices were pondering decisions in cases that had been argued before them.

Chief Justice Fish told Judge Roberts he had been told of the statements attributing the opinion in the land suit to Clayton and asked Judge Roberts if he had ever met Clayton. When Judge Roberts responded in the negative, the chief justice summoned Clayton to the conference room and introduced him to Judge Roberts. Judge Roberts said, "Clayton, I want to apologize to you. I've been doing you a great injustice. I've been saying that you wrote the opinion in my land suit case which bears Chief Justice Fish's name. Since meeting you and seeing what an intelligent-looking man you are, I am convinced that you could not have written that fool opinion."

𝕬 James H. Pou, of Raleigh, was a trial lawyer of much ability and renown. He was an unusually large man, and he habitually sought to minimize the discomfort of summer heat by deliberately and slowly fanning himself with a large palm-leaf fan.

I am indebted to my late friend Sumner Burgwyn for this story. I was privileged to serve in the North Carolina House of Representatives with him and another friend, Clayton Moore. Both Sumner and Clayton afterward sat on the North Carolina Superior Court bench.

Mr. Pou had recently won a jury verdict in a famous case acquitting a wealthy client of murder on the plea of temporary insanity. A few days after this event Sumner and Clayton met in the most politically saturated inn in America, the Sir Walter Hotel in Raleigh. Finding that they both had chores at the state capitol, they undertook to walk along Fayetteville Street together to that historic structure.

En route, Clayton told Sumner about a rumor that Pou had received a fee of unprecedentedly enormous size in the recent case, and Sumner emphatically questioned the truth of the rumor.

Immediately thereafter they met Pou, who was walking along Fayetteville Street in the opposite direction with his perennial fan. After they had exchanged amenities, Clayton said, "We were just arguing about you."

Pou, who was the soul of urbanity, responded, "What was the argument about? Maybe I can settle it. I dislike controversy between gentlemen."

Clayton replied, "We were arguing about what a rumor says concerning your fee in the recent famous trial. Rumor says your fee was seventy-five thousand dollars." He added, "Sumner and I know that the amount of your fee is a confidential matter between you and your client and is none of our business. But it would settle our argument if you would tell us whether the figure named in the rumor is anywhere near the truth."

After fanning himself deliberately and slowly with his palm-leaf fan several times, Pou inquired: "Young gentlemen, can you keep a secret?"

Sumner and Clayton assured him that they could.

Pou thereupon ended the conversation by saying, "And so can I. Good-day."

Chapter 8

More Humor
in the Law

🪝 🪝 🪝

One of the most respected and loved of all the human beings who have called North Carolina home was James L. Webb, of Shelby, father of the late Faye Webb Gardner, the lovely wife of Governor O. Max Gardner, and grandfather of my friend the late Ralph Webb Gardner. Like Abou Ben Adhem, he loved his fellowman.

During his early days at the bar, he served as solicitor (North Carolina's old title for the office of district attorney) of one of the state's most extensive districts. Afterward he was elevated to the post of superior court judge, which he filled in a highly satisfactory manner until his death twenty-six years later.

At that time North Carolina was virtually without local courts other than those of justices of the peace, and the superior courts, the state's trial courts of general jurisdiction, tried all criminal cases except those petty cases in which the punishment could not exceed a fine of fifty dollars or imprisonment for thirty days.

As a consequence of this and the size of his district, Solicitor Webb was required to spend an average of five exhausting days a week carrying the heavy burden of prosecuting without assistance crowded criminal dockets. On Saturdays, he sometimes took one or two drinks and relaxed by meeting and conversing with his legion of friends on the sidewalks in Shelby.

The son of a leading Baptist clergyman of bygone years, Solicitor Webb held membership in the First Baptist Church of Shelby and was a generous contributor to its budget. At a meeting of its deacons, the young pastor, who had recently accepted the call to the church, made this statement: "Brethren, I have just learned that one of our most prominent members, Solicitor Webb, sometimes exhibits himself on the streets in a slightly inebriated state and thus sets a bad example to the community. I suggest as your pastor that one of you ought to remonstrate with Brother Webb and urge him to mend his ways."

A wise old deacon responded, "I've always heard a new broom sweeps cleanest. Preacher, you're a new broom in Shelby. I suggest that you remonstrate with Brother Webb." The pastor promised to do so and to report his action to a meeting of the deacons.

After several meetings had passed without any report from the pastor, the old deacon asked him if he had ever remonstrated with Brother Webb. The pastor replied, "On the first Saturday after I agreed to do so, I found Brother Webb relaxing in his customary way with a group of his friends. After his friends had dispersed one by one, I engaged Brother Webb in conversation. I did not wish to approach my real objective too abruptly. So I said, 'It's sad to realize that winter is near at hand and that many of the poor in our prosperous city will lack adequate food, fuel, and other necessities of life during the inclement weather.'

"Brother Webb," the pastor continued, "thereupon pulled twenty-five dollars in cash [an enormous sum in that day] out of his pocket and handed it to me, saying, 'I'm absent most of the time and don't have many contacts with the needy, who are sure to call on you for help. Use this money for their benefit. Let me know when it's exhausted, and I'll supply you some more.'"

By way of conclusion, the pastor added, "When Brother Webb did that, I decided that he has more religion when he's half drunk than anybody else I know has when he's completely sober, and that it was not my Christian duty to remonstrate with him."

❦   As a superior court judge, James Webb endeared himself to the bar and people of North Carolina by his learning and wisdom. He truly executed justice in mercy. In pronouncing sentences upon pleas and convictions in criminal cases, he distinguished between those who were criminals at heart and those who offended without prior design in response to temptations or provocations of the moment. Those in the last category always received at his hands mercy whose quality was never strained.

Imprinted indelibly in my recollection is the day I represented an old client, named Benton, before Judge Webb in Burke Superior Court.

At that time solicitors received no salaries. Their compensation consisted of fees paid them in cases in which the accused pleaded guilty or they secured convictions. As a consequence, energetic solicitors sought to discover additional cases while they were prosecuting docketed cases, and dockets in their courts were likely to increase rather than decrease as the days passed.

Old man Benton had been caught by the law operating a twenty-gallon copper still in his dwelling house. Since he had no defense, he entered a plea of guilty. As was his right and custom, R. L. Huffman, the solicitor, called Benton to the witness stand, intent on discovering another culprit to prosecute. "Who supplied the still to you?" he inquired. "I ain't gwine to tell you," Benton answered.

After several unsuccessful attempts to extract the identity of the supplier of the still from Benton, the solicitor moved that Judge Webb adjudge Benton guilty of contempt of court and order him jailed until he made the revelation the solicitor sought.

In his quiet judicial manner, Judge Webb said, "Mr. Solicitor, all of us need a code of ethics to guide our perplexed steps through this troublous world. Mr. Benton evidently has devised for himself a code of ethics. It may not be the best code of ethics, but it is the only code he's got. His code forbids him to tell on others. Mr. Benton did not intend to be contemptuous of the court when he said he wasn't going to tell you who supplied him with the still. He merely meant that he didn't want to tell you."

At this point Benton had the temerity to interject, "That's right, Judge. But I ain't gwine to tell him nohow."

After this interruption, Judge Webb continued, "It would be difficult to do a greater injury to any human being than to compel him to violate his code of ethics. The court will not do such an injury to Mr. Benton. Mr. Solicitor, your motion is denied."

I often recalled what Judge Webb so wisely said and ruled on that far distant day when judges in other areas of the nation were jailing journalists for adhering to their code of ethics and declining to reveal the identity of informants and the information they obtained from them. Most of such information, I digress to note, was hearsay which would have been inadmissible in any trial on the merits.

As Judge Webb so well demonstrated, judges need wisdom as well as legal learning, and they add glory to the bench when they exercise their discretion by subordinating the cruelties of the letter of the law to the dictates of wisdom.

❧   Laymen often criticize the bar because so many of the men involved in the Watergate tragedy had been licensed to practice law.

Yet only two of them, John Mitchell, a specialist in bond law, which is an immeasurably small part of the law, and John Ehrlichman, a specialist in zoning law, which is another immeasurably small part of the law, actually practiced law. If either of them ever read the Constitution, he didn't understand it. The others were political lawyers, who knew administrative officials rather than the law.

All of them remind me of what my old friend Marvin Ritch said of himself when he was a candidate for the Democratic nomination for United States senator. Marvin introduced himself to a passer-by and solicited his vote in the forthcoming primary. The passer-by inquired, "Mr. Ritch, what is your profession?" "I'm a lawyer," Marvin replied. The passer-by said, "I can't vote for you. I swore a long time ago I'd never vote for a lawyer for public office." Marvin, who was equal to any emergency, patted the passer-by on the shoulder and assured him, "If that's all you've got against me, you can vote for me with a clear conscience. I'm not enough of a lawyer to hurt."

❧   Julius A. Rousseau, of North Wilkesboro, one of my contemporaries on the North Carolina Superior Court bench, was noted for his self-belittling humor.

Under the state constitution, Supreme Court justices and regular superior court judges are elected in North Carolina by the people for eight-year terms. I praise this system for two reasons: It is in harmony with the assertion of the Declaration of Independence that the just powers of government are derived from the consent of the governed, and it has given North Carolina excellent judges, who are reelected by the people as long as they desire to serve.

When he was running for superior court judge, Jule Rousseau visited Mitchell County, one of the counties in his district, in quest of votes. As he drove along a lonesome road, he saw some laborers at a sawmill. He left his automobile at the roadside, walked to the sawmill, and pleaded with them for their support.

The only encouragement he got was from their foreman, who told him to wait at his automobile until they could caucus. He returned to his car and observed the workers in an agitated huddle. After a few minutes, the foreman came to him and asked, "If you are elected judge, will you hold court at Bakersville?" Jule responded, "Sometimes."

The foreman said, "My boys get caught by the law occasionally operating stills or possessing moonshine. They're interested in who's the judge. They want a judge who's not too bright and can't catch on to everything."

Jule rejoined, "Then I'm your man."

The foreman assured him, "That's what we decided. You can count on our support."

༜ Shortly after he had tried a famous case, Judge Rousseau was holding the superior court of Guilford County. Greensboro's afternoon newspaper received a dispatch from Raleigh stating that the state Supreme Court had that day reversed his ruling in the famous case and sent a reporter to interview him. Judge Rousseau told the reporter, "I'm not going to talk about that case or the Supreme Court. The Supreme Court has reversed me so often I've lost all confidence in its judgment."

༜ My father was a country lawyer who practiced actively for sixty-five years. Like most Southerners of his generation, he was denied a college education by the hard times that prevailed in most areas of the South for many years after the Civil War. He more than surmounted his deprivation by being a voracious reader all of his life. He loved to quote these words from Sir Walter Scott's *Guy*

Mannering: "A lawyer without history or literature is a mechanic, a mere working mason. If he possesses some knowledge of these, he may venture to call himself an architect."

My father studied law without an instructor. After he was admitted to the North Carolina bar in 1879, he read every statute in Battle's *Revisal of the Public Statutes of North Carolina* and every decision in the eighty existing volumes of *The North Carolina Supreme Court Reports*. If he disagreed with the court reporter's analysis of a decision, he wrote his own analysis on the margin of the page of his book.

He always maintained that a lawyer owes to his clients, the courts, the law, and himself the duty to know the facts and the law of his cases, and that cases are won by the diligence of the lawyer in preparing them for trial and not in the courtroom. When I became his law partner, he gave me this instruction on the first duty of a lawyer: "Salt down the facts; the law will keep."

I am indebted to him and my generous friend Richard V. Michaux, sheriff of Burke County, for my acquiring a considerable practice as a trial lawyer soon after I hung out my shingle.

My father, who said he was going to give me an opportunity to make a lawyer of myself if he lost every client he had, briefed me on cases and sent me into court to try them alone. Dick Michaux had legions of friends who sought his advice on all subjects, and he prevaricated to them most eloquently about my nonexistent prowess as a trial lawyer.

Their endeavors were enhanced by the circumstance that I was compelled to absent myself from the first week of the August term of the superior court of Burke County to attend the summer encampment of the North Carolina National Guard. Retired emergency judge C. C. Lyon, of distant Bladen County, had been assigned to hold the August term, which was designed to try criminal cases.

Inasmuch as Judge Lyon was unknown to Burke County sinners and they were hesitant to confront uncertainty of punishment, all of them who had cases scheduled for trial asserted I was their lawyer and asked the court to postpone their trials until the next week so they could be defended by me. Judge Lyon acceded to their requests and recessed court for the week, saying it was the only time he had been compelled to adjourn court because of the absence of one lawyer.

Since all of them had assured the court that I was their attorney, they were necessarily compelled to retain my services before they confronted Judge Lyon during the second week. Incidentally, Judge Lyon endeared himself to Burke County during that August term, was afterward assigned to hold special terms of its superior court on many occasions at the request of its bar, and became one of my favorite judges.

   The practice of law today is a far cry from what it was then. Shysters were few in number, and lawyers in general occupied a status on a par with ministers and physicians. They did not specialize. On the contrary, they accepted retainers from clients in all walks of law and tried both civil and criminal cases, whether they were significant or petty.

Organized crime was nonexistent, and burglaries were unknown. Householders did not even bother to lock their doors at night. Larceny was seldom committed, because people in general deemed thieves to be earth's most contemptible creatures. Since men were prone to drink and fight, crimes involving liquor and violence occupied substantial space on court dockets. The propensity for drinking explains why so many humorous stories of that day are concerned with liquor.

Humorous incidents that occurred during my days as a practicing lawyer are past numbering. I shall nevertheless mention only two of them as exceptions to the rules I made for my guidance in writing of humor in law.

The first is inconsistent with my father's frequently iterated assertion that cases are won by the prior preparatory work of the lawyer and not in the courtroom.

My beloved friend John Mull was substituting for the solicitor and prosecuting my client Bush Clark in Burke Superior Court on an indictment charging him with the larceny of four automobile tires from John D. Orders, a respectable Burke County farmer. Mull owned a large ornate pocket watch, which was a prized heirloom.

Although he had never been suspected of larceny or any other crime involving moral turpitude before, Bush Clark had a rather lengthy criminal record, and he and I shared the belief that it would endanger his chance of an acquittal if he took the witness stand to deny his guilt of the pending charge and thereby subjected himself to cross-examination respecting his past.

As the only witness for the prosecution, John Orders told the jury that a year before he had bought four new automobile tires, which he had made identifiable by him by scratching crossmarks on them with his pocket knife. The tires disappeared from his premises before he had installed them on his automobile. About eight months later he saw the tires on the wheels of Bush Clark's car, which was standing beside the curb, but before he could lay claim to the tires Bush drove away, and he had not seen them since.

Since Bush did not take the witness stand, I was entitled to the closing argument to the jury. As it was nearing the end of the court day, Mull and I agreed to limit our arguments to the jury severely. To confine them to the stipulated time, Mull placed his ornate pocket watch on a nearby table, and I put my nondescript pocket watch beside it.

When Mr. Mull finished his argument to the jury, he picked up my watch, put it in his watch pocket, and seated himself within the bar. I thereupon told the jury that Brother Mull had made a powerful argument in respect to the ability of John Orders to identify the tires, but that his subsequent action had spoken more convincingly than his words. "He has inadvertently appropriated my watch," I said.

Mull pulled my watch out of his pocket and said, "I'm sorry. I did take your watch."

I thereupon ended my remarks to the jury by saying, "Brother Mull has undoubtedly looked at his beautiful watch scores of times daily over a period of years to ascertain the time of day. If a smart man like Brother Mull, with such vast opportunities to know his own watch, could make a mistake as to its identity, as he has, then John Orders, who merely saw the tires on Bush Clark's car for one fleeting second, could be mistaken in his identification of them."

The jury speedily acquitted Bush.

❦ I defended Dick Breeden, who processed chickens for market, before United States District Judge Johnson J. Hayes and a jury in the district court during the Second World War on the charge of paying a dealer in poultry more than the price fixed by the regulations of the Office of Price Administration.

When the district attorney rested his case, Judge Hayes excused the jury from the courtroom at my request and I moved for a directed verdict of innocence because of my conviction that the government's evidence was insufficient to justify a verdict of guilty.

During my argument on the motion, Judge Hayes interjected, "Your client's offense, if any, seems to have been more inadvertent than intentional. If he will enter a plea of *nolo contendere*, I will let him go without any restrictions whatever upon the payment of a fine of two hundred dollars."

As a lawyer, I was sometimes persistent in presenting my arguments to the court. Judge Hayes interrupted me a second time, saying, "Perhaps you should take your client outside the courtroom and talk to him privately."

I did. Dick said, "I've got great confidence in you as a lawyer. Otherwise, I wouldn't have retained you. If you should happen to be mistaken about the law in this case and somebody has to go to jail, it will be me and not you. I'd rather pay the two hundred and go on my way."

❦ Judge Hayes was a forthright judge. Trying without a jury a civil case which the United States had brought against a private corporation, he ruled in favor of the private corporation. The government was represented by a rather officious attorney from the Department of Justice, who vociferously exclaimed, "What am I to tell the Department of Justice about this?" Judge Hayes remarked, "You could tell the department that you lost the case."

❦ The Board of Commissioners of Burke County established the Burke County Criminal Court in 1935 and appointed me its first judge. The court had jurisdiction to try ordinary misdemeanors on their merits, and its judge was permitted to appear as a lawyer in cases not coming before it.

In retrospect, I find satisfaction in my service as its judge. Although any accused had the legal right to demand that the facts be determined by a jury rather than the judge, none of them ever did. Furthermore, there were few appeals to the superior court from my judgments.

The most humorous incident during my judgeship involved Sherman Lail, an ardent Democrat, who was a chronic visitor to the court on charges of public drunkenness. Sherman always pleaded guilty and usually accepted the court's rulings without murmur.

About two weeks before the election of 1936 he appeared in the Burke County Criminal Court on the usual charge and entered his usual plea of guilty.

I said, "Sherman, you're a great trial to this court. It has tried everything in its repertoire on you and nothing keeps you sober." Sherman responded, "Your Honor, you've never tested me with a suspended sentence." I inquired, "Sherman, if I were to give you a suspended sentence, do you think it would do any good?" Sherman rejoined, "If you don't require me to keep sober too long."

I said, "I'm going to accept your suggestion. I will give you a suspended sentence on condition you stay sober until Christmas Eve. If you will stay sober to that time and not do any injury to anybody or anything, I'll not do anything with you if you happen to slip up and get drunk on Christmas Eve."

I observed my good friend the Reverend J. C. Cornett, pastor of the Morganton Methodist Church, grinning at me, and added, "Sherman, I'm not encouraging you to get drunk on Christmas Eve. I'm trying to keep you sober until that time."

Sherman promised to stay sober until Christmas Eve, and I gave him the suspended sentence.

On election day Franklin D. Roosevelt carried all the states except Maine and Vermont, and on election night Sherman got publicly drunk.

On his appearance before the court the following week on the usual charge, Sherman entered his usual plea of guilty. "Sherman," I said, "you promised me to stay sober until Christmas Eve if I gave you a suspended sentence, and you got drunk on election night."

For the first time Sherman undertook to justify his sin. He said,

"Your Honor, I've never offered any excuse for my misconduct before. But I'm not to blame this time. When I heard how the election had gone, it sounded like Santa Claus had come, and I thought it would be all right for me to get drunk."

ϟ   Governor Clyde R. Hoey appointed me a special superior court judge on January 11, 1937, and I served in that capacity under subsequent appointments made by him and his successor, Governor Joseph Melville Broughton, until December 31, 1943, when I resigned and resumed the practice of law.

During those seven years, I spent about forty-two weeks a year trying jury cases in some forty-five of the state's one hundred counties, met the local officials in those forty-five counties, and became acquainted with virtually all of the lawyers in the state.

I will note only a few of the humorous incidents I encountered as a superior court judge.

ϟ   Years before the Supreme Court of the United States put its liberal interpretation on the Sixth Amendment's guaranty of the right of counsel to the accused in criminal cases, I became convinced that a layman is unable to secure a fair trial in a criminal case unless he is represented by a lawyer. As a superior court judge, I always asked an accused who was without an attorney if he wished the court to assign a lawyer to defend him. If he answered me in the affirmative, I requested an attorney to defend him without compensation, and my request was never refused. A young man appeared before me without a lawyer in the superior court of Lenoir County. When I put my customary question to him, he replied, "No, Your Honor, I don't need a lawyer. I'm going to plead guilty and throw myself on the ignorance of the court."

ϟ   In accordance with an essential practice, I afforded those who had been summoned to serve as grand and petit jurors in the superior court of Rutherford County an opportunity to present excuses as to why they thought they should be exempt from serving. Grand jurors do not try cases on their merits. They listen to witnesses produced before them in secret session at the instance of the prosecution and determine from their testimony whether there is probable cause to believe the accused to be guilty and whether the accused should be put on trial before petit jurors in open court.

One of the panel of jurors presented the excuse that he was totally deaf in one ear and exceedingly hard of hearing in the other. Being suspicious of the validity of his claim I asked him a number of questions and in so doing lowered my voice to almost a whisper. I discovered that although he had a slight impairment of hearing in one ear, he had acute hearing in the other.

In refusing to excuse him, I said, "You have at least one good ear. You may be one of the eighteen members of the panel who are drawn to serve on the grand jury. If so, your good ear will permit you to hear everything it is necessary for you to hear. After all, grand jurors only have to hear one side of the question—the prosecution side."

❦   Ed Hege, a farmer of Davidson County, left a substantial estate and a multitude of dissatisfied relatives. About a dozen of them sued his administrator for large sums in separate actions under complaints alleging that they had always been solicitous of his welfare and had rendered many services to him during his twilight years on his implied promises to compensate them for so doing. Zenobian I. Walser, who was usually called Nobe and who was an adroit trial lawyer, was counsel for Ed Hege's administrator.

I was the presiding judge at a term of the superior court of Davidson County when the cases were tried. By consent of the parties, they were consolidated for trial by the jury. When he summed up the administrator's case, Nobe added up the claims of all the plaintiffs on a blackboard before the jury. Pointing to their total, which was enormous, Nobe said, "Gentlemen of the jury, Ed Hege is dead. He is in heaven. If his kinfolks were half as good to him in his declining years as they claim, Ed Hege made a sorry trade when he swapped earth for heaven."

❦   I held a criminal term of the superior court of Johnston County at which a prisoner whose name has escaped my memory was scheduled to be tried for a capital offense. The solicitor of the district was Claude Canaday, who had been a college-mate of mine at Chapel Hill.

When the sheriff brought the prisoner into the courtroom at the solicitor's request for the purpose of a motion, I noticed that he was wearing a bushy beard. The solicitor informed the court that the prisoner had always been smooth-shaven in times past, alleged that he had grown the beard to feign insanity, and moved that the court enter an order directing the sheriff to have him shaved.

In denying the motion, I said, "The Constitution gives everybody the right to hide behind the Fifth Amendment. I don't know any legal principle which forbids an accused to hide behind a beard."

❧   In holding superior court, I sought to preside "with the cold neutrality of an impartial judge." Candor compels me to confess, however, that I did not do so when Henry Fisher, the assistant solicitor, was prosecuting Colonel Thomas L. Kirkpatrick's somewhat aged client in the superior court of Mecklenburg County on the charge of driving an automobile one Sunday afternoon on a public street in Pineville while under the influence of an intoxicating beverage.

The colonel was one of North Carolina's most spectacular legal and political figures. When President Woodrow Wilson visited Charlotte to make a public speech, Colonel Kirkpatrick, as mayor, used forty-five minutes introducing him, and President Wilson spoke for twelve minutes.

A policeman of Pineville testified before the jury that on a Sunday afternoon the accused drove an automobile loaded with a multitude of passengers in a zigzag fashion on the public street of the town, and that when he stopped the automobile, he detected what he took to be the odor of alcohol on the accused's breath.

The accused testified that he was a teetotaler. He had been a patient at Mecklenburg Sanatorium many years before, he said, and the physician at that institution advised him at the time of his discharge never to drink strong drink, advice he had heeded ever since. He and his passengers had been en route home from church when he was stopped. He had difficulty getting tires for his automobile in those tire-rationing days, and in consequence he had a big tire on his right front wheel and a little tire on his left front wheel. His automobile undoubtedly traveled in a zigzag fashion, he concluded, because the little tire pulled it to his left, and he had to jerk it back to the right.

On his cross-examination, Henry Fisher asked one question too many. He noted that the accused had testified he was on his way home from church and demanded that he tell the court and jury what was the text of the sermon he had heard.

Quick as a flash, the accused said, "The minister preached on a text from the Book of Nahum, which says, 'The Lord is slow to anger, and great in power, and will not at all acquit the wicked.'"

I had forgotten that the exceedingly short Book of Nahum was in the Bible. I read the book that evening in the Gideon Bible in my hotel room and observed that it spoke of the jumping chariots that frequented the streets of Nineveh.

After Henry Fisher and Colonel Kirkpatrick concluded their arguments to the jury the next morning, I delivered to it an unorthodox charge. As nearly as I can reconstruct it from memory, it was as follows.

"Gentlemen of the Jury: In order that my charge may harmonize with the Book of Nahum, I will use the term 'jumping chariot' to mean an automobile. The state charges that the accused drove a jumping chariot on the public street of Pineville on the Sabbath Day while he was under the influence of some intoxicating beverage. The accused admits that the state makes such charge against him in legal language, but contends that in so doing the state is emulating the Comforters of Job and multiplying words without knowledge.

"The accused further contends that he has not imbibed a single drop of an alcoholic beverage since he was discharged from the Mecklenburg Sanatorium many years ago; that he has not even heeded St. Paul's advice to 'use a little wine for thy stomach's sake and thine often infirmities' since that time; and that he has not even looked upon the wine 'when it is red' and 'giveth its colour in the cup' since that time. He further contends that he listened with complete sobriety to the sermon on the text from the Book of Nahum, and when it asserts that the Lord 'will not at all acquit the wicked,' the text implies that the Lord will not permit the righteous to be convicted. I charge you that if the state has satisfied you not only beyond a reasonable doubt, but beyond all doubt, that the accused drove a jumping chariot on a public street in Pineville while under the influence of an intoxicating beverage, you will return a verdict of guilty. But if you are satisfied that the accused was sober enough at the time named in the indictment to remember correctly the text of the preacher's sermon, you will return a verdict of not guilty."

The jury acquitted the accused. I am satisfied that my sole departure from judicial orthodoxy did not deprive justice of its rightful prey.

❧   I had the priceless privilege as a superior court judge to hold a number of criminal terms with John M. Queen, solicitor of the extensive district that stretched from Haywood County on the east through Cherokee County on the west.

Although he was well educated at the university in Chapel Hill, John Queen always spoke the vernacular and liked to delude strangers into believing him to be uneducated. When he held his first courts west of Asheville and met John for the first time, Superior Court Judge John H. Clement made this observation, "John Queen is naturally a smart man. It's a pity he didn't have the advantage of an education."

John was the most spectacular person I have ever known. If a writer could have caught him and imprisoned him within the covers of a book, the book would have been a best-seller. The stories about him are legion. Considerations of space and time compel me to confine mine to two, one which was related to me by Judge John M. Oglesby and another which I acquired by personal observation.

John Queen relished kidding his friends. One of those he loved most and kidded most frequently was Jasper Newton Moody, an able attorney of irreproachable character who had a large practice west of Asheville.

A notorious case in which the prisoner was charged with first-degree murder was called up for trial before Judge Oglesby in the superior court of Graham County, which at that time had a wooden courthouse and sat in the county seat, Robbinsville, where places for the overnight accommodation of guests were virtually nonexistent.

The first day of the term was spent selecting a petit jury to try the murder case. As solicitor, John was the chief counsel for the prosecution, and his friend J. N. Moody, who was usually called Newt, headed the lawyers for the defense.

From time immemorial it has been the practice in North Carolina to put the petit jurors in capital cases under the supervision of a bailiff and keep them in seclusion during their out-of-court hours.

After the petit jurors had been selected, the all-important question arose as to where they could be secluded overnight. One court official or lawyer after another made suggestions which proved to be unfeasible. Judge Oglesby then addressed John Queen. "Mr. Solicitor," he said, "you have been silent during the discussion. The court would be pleased to have a suggestion from you."

John Queen responded, "As I understand it, petit jurors are locked up overnight to keep anyone from tampering with them. The court has a simple solution for its present problem. Lock Newt Moody up, and let the jurors go home."

As solicitor, John Queen prosecuted an accused on a charge of second-degree murder before me as presiding judge and a petit jury in the superior court of Macon County. The accused pleaded self-defense. After a hard-fought trial, the jurors returned a verdict of not guilty.

While they were still seated in the jury box, a man entered the bar of the court and told John that he had signed an appearance bond for a youth charged with operating an illegal distillery and that the youth had failed to appear for trial. He asked John to refrain from seeking a forfeiture of the bond before the next day, for he had discovered where the youth was hiding and believed he could catch him and bring him to court the next day.

On some occasions, John would shout so loudly he could be heard hundreds of yards away. Notwithstanding the bondsman was standing beside him, John shouted, "Bring that young man in. We have a merciful judge presiding. The young fellow is not charged with any serious offense like murder."

Turning to the jurors who had just returned the not-guilty verdict, John said in a more subdued tone of voice, "Gentlemen, murder is a crime in some counties. But not in Macon."

❧   Wilson Warlick, of Newton, North Carolina, adorned the North Carolina superior court bench and the United States District Court judgeship for the Western District of North Carolina successively for almost fifty years.

On the bench he was respected by all for his legal learning, his judicial impartiality, and his compassionate heart. Off the bench he was loved by all for his congeniality, his captivating sense of humor, and his concern for his friends and acquaintances.

Despite the dignity with which he presided in court, he was often called by his childhood nickname "Coot" Warlick by those who remembered the days of his youth and those who were so fortunate as to be his most intimate friends.

During his childhood, Judge Warlick often visited his uncle Andrew Wilson, a substantial Catawba County farmer, and played and fished with a black of the same age, who was named Coulter and was the son of one of his uncle's tenants.

Years later Coulter's name appeared on the docket of the superior court of Catawba County as a defendant charged with illegally possessing some moonshine whiskey. Spurgeon Spurling was the prosecuting attorney, and Judge Warlick was the presiding judge at the term of court at which Coulter's case was scheduled for trial.

Coulter appeared without a lawyer. Spurling, who did not know Coulter from Adam, asked him, "Don't you want a lawyer?"

Coulter replied, "Thank you, sir. I don't need a lawyer. I'm expecting Judge 'Coot' to look after me."

Judge Coot tempered the wind to Coulter, just as he did to many other shorn lambs, black and white, who stood before him during his years on the bench.

❧   North Carolina has been inseparably wedded since its beginning to the beliefs that trial by jury is the surest bulwark of liberty and that jurors should never be the unthinking echoes of the judge's opinion as to questions of fact. To this end, North Carolina has had at all times since 1796 a statute which states that in giving his charge to the jury a judge must state the facts given in evidence and explain impartially the law to them, but must not indicate by word, gesture, or otherwise any opinion as to whether any fact has been proven.

Judge Warlick exhibited his fidelity to this statute at all times. He was criticized by a litigant on one occasion for so doing.

My friend John C. Stroupe, of the Hickory, North Carolina, bar, represented the plaintiff in a civil action which was tried by Judge Warlick and a jury in the superior court of Catawba County.

While Judge Warlick was explaining his contentions to the jury, the plaintiff tugged John's coattail and whispered in his ear, "The judge is certainly a fair man." Pursuant to his judicial duty of impartiality, Judge Warlick began to state the contentions of the defendant to the jury. The plaintiff thereupon tugged John's coattails a second time and whispered in his ear, "That damned judge is two-faced."

❦   Judge Warlick and I often spoke to the same audiences. After we had both passed the age of four-score years, we were speakers at a happy occasion celebrating the retirement from business of our mutual friend Lloyd Mullinax. When the master of ceremonies introduced Judge Warlick, he noted that both speakers were above four-score years of age. Judge Warlick responded, "That's true. If I had anticipated I would live so long, I would have taken better care of myself when I was young."

Judge Warlick suffered a fatal accident without fault on his part at the hands of a driver whose truck struck an automobile in which he was a passenger while it was standing at an intersection awaiting a change of traffic signals.

I often think of Judge Warlick. When I do, I always recall what Fitz-Greene Hallack said of his departed friend Joseph Rodman Drake.

> Green be the turf about thee,
> Friend of my better days!
> None knew thee but to love thee,
> Nor named thee but to praise.

❦   During my occupancy of the office of superior court judge, I presided over numerous terms of the superior court of Mecklenburg County. On one occasion, John G. Carpenter, the prosecuting attorney, prosecuted a rare character known as "the Professor," who was indicted for supplying a pregnant woman with a substance to induce her miscarriage.

All of the substance had disappeared, and its nature had never been determined by an analysis. Hence, the case for the prosecution was not strong.

The Professor, who had an uncanny capacity to smile benignly under all circumstances, really demolished the prosecution's case by testifying, "I didn't supply the lady with anything except a love powder. She wanted it to put in the coffee of the young fellow who was responsible for her condition, and make him love and marry her and legitimize her child-to-be."

After the Professor gave this testimony, Carpenter plied him with many questions designed to impeach his credibility. The Professor smiled benignly, and denied all the incriminating insinuations. Finally John put this question to him: "I ask you, Professor, if you didn't desert your first wife in Mecklenburg County many years ago, go to Gaston County, enter into a second marriage with a Gaston County woman without getting a divorce from your first wife, live with the Gaston County woman for years, have three children by her, and then desert her and the three children?"

The Professor smiled benignly, and answered, "Mr. Carpenter, if I ever did any such outrageous things, I've forgotten all about them."

A witness may find a convenient forgettery more useful than a good memory.

Chapter 9

Humor
in the
Legislature

ও ও ও

n June 1922, as I was taking my first-year examinations in my third year at Harvard Law School, I was surprised to receive a telegram from Charles F. Kirksey, chairman of the Burke County Democrats, stating that the Democratic county convention had named me its candidate for Burke County's seat in the North Carolina House of Representatives. After I was elected to this post in the ensuing election in November, my old friend Lum Garrison gave me this sage counsel: "When you go to the legislature, pass no more laws, and 'peal half of those we've already got." If federal and state legislators had been as wise as Lum Garrison during recent years, Americans would not be the law-ridden people they are.

I was subsequently reelected to the North Carolina House in 1924 and 1930 and had the privilege altogether of serving in the General Assemblies of 1923, 1925, and 1931 with many outstanding North Carolinians. Among them were college-mates at Chapel Hill, Victor S. Bryant, Floyd Crouse, Harley Black Gaston, Carlisle W. Higgins, and James S. Howell; three able speakers, John G. Dawson, Edgar W. Pharr, and Willis Smith; Lindsay C. Warren, who became comptroller general of the United States; Gregg Cherry, who was afterward chosen governor of North Carolina; and Aaron A. F. Seawell, who subsequently served as North Carolina's attorney general and justice of her Supreme Court. Like everything I have ever done, my service in the North Carolina Legislature was fascinating, and I made many enduring friendships.

North Carolina's state senators and representatives were moved to serve by patriotism, not by the emoluments of their offices. In 1923 and 1925 they drew four dollars a day for not exceeding sixty days, and their only fringe benefit was reimbursement for one round trip between their homes and the state capital. Prior to the 1931 session, however, their compensation was increased to ten dollars a day for sixty days.

❦   The Supreme Court's one-man, one-vote ruling harmonizes with democracy. While it operates justly in a single political subdivision, the ruling produces at times unfortunate repercussions when the redistricting of congressional districts, state senatorial districts, and legislative districts compels a state legislature to assign heavily populated and sparsely settled subdivisions to the same district to satisfy its mandate. This is so because the majority of voters are prone to elect to public offices inhabitants of the heavily populated areas rather than wiser men and women dwelling in the sparsely settled ones.

Alleghany County is a mountainous county of small population in northwestern North Carolina. Rufus A. Doughton, his brother Robert L. Doughton, Carlisle Higgins, and Floyd Crouse first came to the appreciative knowledge of North Carolinians while representing Alleghany in the North Carolina Legislature. Subsequently, Rufus Doughton, Carlisle Higgins, and Floyd Crouse took high rank among the state's ablest public servants in statewide offices, and Robert L. Doughton acquired national fame serving with wisdom as "Farmer Bob" Doughton, chairman of the House Ways and Means Committee in Washington.

If the one-man, one-vote rule had been in vogue when they began their political careers, their talents might have been hidden from public view in big districts drawn to comply with the mandate of the rule, and they might have died unhonored and unsung and left North Carolina and America bereft of their wise public services.

Farmer Bob Doughton possessed a practical understanding of economics of far more value than the theoretical knowledge of the professional economists who undertake to advise federal officials. Acting at the suggestion of his professional economists, who believed high income taxes to be an antidote for inflation, the secretary of the Treasury sent a proposed revenue bill making drastic increases in federal income taxes to Farmer Bob with the request that he introduce it in the House with his blessing as chairman of the House Ways and Means Committee.

When he heard nothing from Congressman Doughton concerning the bill, the secretary called him by telephone and asked him when he was going to introduce the bill. "I ain't never going to introduce that fool bill," Farmer Bob responded. "Don't your economists have enough sense to know that you can shear a sheep every spring, but you can't skin him but once?"

I share Farmer Bob's misgiving in respect to high taxes as an antidote for inflation. I suspect they are rather a stimulant for that economic ailment. When Congress substantially increased federal income taxes while I was last practicing law, I could not decrease my office expenses accordingly. I had to charge my clients bigger fees to meet my increased taxes, and discovered that the suppliers of my needs had to charge me bigger prices for their goods and services to meet theirs. I am tempted to believe, therefore, that the United States government might be operated with more wisdom if it were more economical in taking advice from professional economists.

❧   Farmer Bob Doughton told me a story which congressmen who are accustomed to polling their constituents to ascertain how they should vote ought to heed. When he first went to the House, Farmer Bob wrote letters to constituents whose views he respected, asking them how they thought he ought to vote on crucial issues. He desisted from his practice, however, on receiving the following reply from an Ashe County farmer.

"Bob Doughton, I've got my spring plowing to do, and I can't spend my time telling you how to vote. We elected you to Congress at a big salary to study these questions and vote on them in the way you think best for us. If you're too dumb or too lazy to do that, come home and we'll send somebody else to Congress in your place."

❧   Zeb Vance became a candidate for Buncombe County's seat in the North Carolina House of Representatives at an early age. His adversary was an elderly gentleman. They met in debate at the courthouse in Asheville. Vance's adversary spoke first. He assured the audience that his young opponent's character was good, and that he would say nothing derogatory about it. He strenuously insisted, however, that the voters should cast their ballots for him because Vance was too young and inexperienced to represent Buncombe County at Raleigh.

In replying, Vance said, "It would not be fair for you to hold me responsible for my youth. Except for those unhappy people who commit suicide, nobody has anything to do with the time of his entrance into the world or his exit from it. The campaign's on, and the time for candidates to make political promises is here. I'm going to make you a political promise, which, unlike many political promises, will be kept. If you will overlook my youth and inexperience this time and send me to the legislature, I'll never be so young and inexperienced again as long as I live."

Vance was elected.

A Democratic member twitted Mose Harshaw, the Republican representative from Caldwell County, for taking a position in debate incompatible with his party's platform. Mose, whose political instincts prompted him to speak in ungrammatical vernacular, responded, "Mr. Speaker, I'm sorry the gentleman isn't smart enough to know that platforms is writ to git in on—not to stand on."

As lieutenant governor of North Carolina, Will Newland was the presiding officer of the North Carolina State Senate in 1911. Just before the Senate session began, Governor Newland procured a patronage position on its staff to reward Moulton Clark, one of Burke County's most faithful Democrats, for his long service to the party.

On his arrival at the state capitol, Uncle Moult, as he was called, looked up Governor Newland, asked him for instructions, and expressed the hope that he would be able to discharge the duties of his position in a satisfying manner. Governor Newland said, "Moult, you'll have no trouble. I got you what legislative critics call a sinecure. All you've got to do is to remind another fellow when it's time to wind the eight-day clock."

❧   As Burke County's representative in the General Assembly of 1911, Joseph F. Spainhour sponsored a local law which made it unlawful to hunt rabbits, a rapidly multiplying species, in Burke County for five years. The law aroused much displeasure among those who enjoyed hunting and those who resented having their vegetable gardens raided by hungry rabbits.

Uncle Joe Allman expressed his displeasure with his accustomed humor. He said, "I was walking from Quaker Meadows to Morganton this morning. An arrogant rabbit ran into the road ahead of me, stood up on his hind legs, and thumbed his nose at me. I picked up a rock to throw at the rabbit, but didn't dare to throw it because the rabbit threatened me. The rabbit said, 'Joe Allman, if you throw that rock at me, I'll tell Joe Spainhour on you.'"

❧   Sir Walter Raleigh's colony lived on Roanoke Island, in North Carolina's coastal waters, before it disappeared and became the Lost Colony, one of the unrevealed mysteries of history. Many years later Roanoke Island became a part of Dare County.

Burge Crisp, a native of Caldwell County, disobeyed Horace Greeley's injunction, "Go west, young man." He went east and settled at Manteo, the county seat of Dare County on Roanoke Island, and was for a time the only lawyer practicing there.

William O. Saunders, the courageous, intelligent, and respected editor of the *Elizabeth City Independent*, published an item which gave umbrage to one of Crisp's clients. Crisp brought a suit for libel against Saunders in behalf of the aggrieved party. I do not know what happened in the libel suit, but I do know it caused a permanent rift between Crisp and Saunders, and nobody thereafter ever accused them of being friends.

At an ensuing term of the North Carolina Legislature, Crisp represented Dare County and his enemy Saunders represented Pasquotank County, of which Elizabeth City was county seat, in the House.

Crisp, who sometimes imbibed hard liquor too freely, staggered into the House during an unusual night session in a visibly intoxicated state and took his seat. Saunders arose and denounced Crisp for appearing in the House in such a deplorable condition. Crisp stood up, held on to his desk to keep from falling, and declared, "Mr. Speaker, the representative from Pasquotank—I won't offend the truth by calling him the gentleman from Pasquotank—ought not have made his cruel statement about me. I'm compelled to confess, however, that for once the representative from Pasquotank has accidentally told the truth. There is nevertheless a happy distinction between him and me. I'm drunk. That's temporary. He's a damned fool. And that's permanent."

❧   State Senator Harry W. Stubbs of Martin County was a perennial member of the General Assembly. If truth is told concerning him, he anticipated by many years those members of the Congress whose contempt for sound economics is largely responsible for the inflation which is bedeviling our land. When he was asked the secret for his immunity to defeat at the polls, Senator Stubbs is reported to have said, "I advocate all appropriations which are sought and oppose all taxes which are proposed."

❧   The Eighteenth Amendment was ratified in 1919. It is difficult to recreate the political climate that prevailed at that time. Ardent advocates of prohibition were obsessed by a zeal which bordered on fanaticism. They supported politicians who voted to outlaw liquor, no matter how much of it they privately consumed, and spurned politicians who voted against prohibition, no matter how sober they were personally. Even some judges, who were supposed to exercise justice in mercy, boycotted mercy in their courtrooms when they sentenced liquor law violators. As a consequence, my father, an outspoken critic of sumptuary laws, was wont to say that John Barleycorn had more enemies in public and more friends in private than any other gentleman of his acquaintance.

In after years a discerning commentator expressed the opinion that Wayne B. Wheeler, longtime general counsel of the Anti-Saloon League, made the Eighteenth Amendment, its implementing Volstead Act, and drastic state prohibition laws possible by establishing the proposition that it was morally respectable for politicians to drink wet as long as they voted dry.

❧   Representative Zeb V. Turlington, of Iredell County, a most conscientious legislator, introduced a bill in the House in 1923 which speedily became law as the Turlington Act. This bill made it a crime for any person to possess within the borders of the state a single drop of any intoxicating beverage. This drastic provision was subject to this solitary exception: it was lawful for a householder to have liquor within his own home for the "bona fide" consumption of himself and his guests in it. Inasmuch as other provisions of the bill made it unlawful for anyone to make, buy, sell, or transport liquor under any circumstances, or to possess it outside his home, it beggars the imagination to conjecture how the bill's sponsors contemplated a householder could obtain any liquor for the "bona fide" consumption of himself and his guests within his home. Maybe they did not intend for him to do so.

Many members of the House deemed the Turlington bill intemperate and unenforceable, and told me that they would vote to kill it without debate if any foolhardy colleague made a tabling motion.

I was prepared to do that. In addition to being a legislative fool who is prone to rush in where legislative angels fear to tread, I suffer from earth's worst affliction, a Scotch-Irish conscience, which commands me to act in accordance with my convictions.

The Turlington proposal violated the truth taught by Sir William Blackstone in his *Commentaries on the Laws of England* that government cannot enforce any law with effectiveness unless the general public favors it. I did not believe the majority of our people really favored the proposal. Moreover, I anticipated, as experience afterward demonstrated, that the proposal, if enacted, would promote hypocrisy in law enforcement because its drastic provisions would be invoked to punish the humble and the weak for their transgressions and ignored insofar as the sins of the prominent and the powerful were concerned.

When I moved to table the Turlington bill, its proponents demanded a roll-call vote. The tabulation of the vote revealed that Julius Brown, of Pitt County, and Victor S. Bryant, of Durham County, had joined me in voting for my tabling motion and that the other 107 representatives in attendance had voted against it.

King David once declared in his wrath that all men are liars. I did not make any statement on that subject, although I knew that many of my colleagues in the House qualified for that description when they voted on my motion to table the Turlington bill.

After the bill passed the House, the Senate chamber and the corridors adjacent to it in the state capitol resounded for several days with fiery speeches of senators urging the Senate to join the House and make the Turlington bill law.

Becoming wearied by the oratory, Rufus L. Haymore, a redoubtable old Republican senator from Surry County, arose and said, "Mr. President, the Senate ought to quit wasting time. Everybody knows the Senate is going to approve the bill because there are fifty hypocrites in the Senate and I'm one of them. We ought to pass the bill, take a recess, whet our appetites with some good old moonshine, and go to lunch."

Whether the Senate took Rufus Haymore's admonition totally I do not know. But I do know that shortly after he uttered it, the Senate converted the Turlington bill into the Turlington Act.

෪   In discussing the nature and uses of humor, I referred briefly to the bill to prohibit the teaching of evolution in the public colleges and schools of the state. This bill, which was authored by Representative David Scott Poole, of Hoke County, provoked the most bitter legislative battle in the 1925 House.

As is true in respect to prohibition, it is not easy to reconstruct the political climate surrounding the Poole bill. The proposal had the strong backing of multitudes of fundamentalists throughout the state. Some of them apparently feared that Christianity would vanish from North Carolina if the teaching of evolution were not outlawed.

Those of us who deplored the attitude of mind the bill revealed were much heartened in our efforts to defeat it by illuminating statements of Harry Woodhouse Chase, president of the University of North Carolina, and William Louis Poteat, president of Wake Forest University, to the effect that the bill was designed to impose tyranny on the minds of North Carolinians and to destroy academic freedom in the state.

The most powerful foes of the Poole bill in the House were Henry

G. Connor, Jr., of Wilson County, and Walter Murphy, of Rowan. Walter Murphy, who bore the nickname Pete, was as valuable a state legislator as North Carolina has ever had. During his long service, he had the daring to advocate substantial appropriations for the state's educational institutions, no matter how financially bleak the times were. As a keen student of government, history, and literature, he spoke with eloquence and enlightenment.

As a citizen, lawyer, judge, and legislator, I have heard speeches, good, bad, and indifferent, on occasions and subjects past numbering. I am constrained to say in retrospect that Murphy's well-prepared and delivered speech against the Poole bill was the most magnificent and telling oration I have ever heard. He portrayed the bill in matchless words as a foolish and futile legislative attempt to limit the bounds of human thought. The speeches of North Carolina legislators are not recorded, and his remarks on the Poole bill have largely been lost to history. They undoubtedly clinched the bill's defeat.

Although he was noted for his gentility, Murphy occasionally resorted to sledgehammer tactics in debate. In his speech on the Poole bill he stated that he had read what Charles Darwin and Herbert Spencer had written on evolution and had found nothing in it which was antagonistic to religion. One of the bill's strongest advocates put to him this question: "Doesn't the reading of such books have a disastrous impact on one's religious faith?" Murphy replied, "In my opinion anyone whose religious faith is disastrously affected by reading Darwin and Spencer hasn't got the intelligence of an anthropoid ape." On another occasion a House member charged that Murphy had insinuated in a colloquy between them that the member did not understand his own bill. By way of reply, Murphy said, "Mr. Speaker, I did not insinuate anything. I stated positively that the gentleman is as ignorant of the implications of his bill as an alley cat is of birth control."

❧   Murphy was the chairman of the Appropriations Committee in the 1925 House. After much penny-pinching, he and his committeemen presented an appropriation bill to the House which harmonized with anticipated revenues and promised a balanced state budget for the next biennium. While the House was considering the bill, a member presented a proposed amendment which would have thrown the budget out of balance if it had been adopted.

The amendment had substantial vote-getting appeal. It proposed substantial increases in the pensions that the state was paying to the surviving Confederate veterans and the widows of those Confederates who had already pitched their tents on fame's eternal camping ground.

Murphy made a speech in opposition to the amendment which brought tears to the eyes of many of those who heard it. After describing in words of incomparable beauty the valor Confederates displayed on land and sea in the Civil War, he asserted that the veterans of all wars except Confederate veterans had plundered public treasuries in quest of larger pensions and implored the House not to insult the surviving Confederate veterans and the memories of their departed comrades by raiding the state's treasury in their names. With tears streaming down the faces of many of its members, the House rejected the amendment and kept the budget in balance.

🦌 Republicanism is dominant in mountainous Mitchell County, where adherents of that party are many and Democrats are few. While it may have been the concoction of a slanderous Democrat, a story of First World War origin has been cited by some to indicate the strength of Mitchell's Republicanism.

After America entered the war against Germany, President Woodrow Wilson assured her people with his customary eloquence that they were fighting the war to make the world safe for democracy. Sometime later a Mitchell youth was charged with failing to register for the draft. He undertook to justify his dereliction by this assertion: "I'm not supposed to fight in this war. The President says it's a war to make the world safe for Democrats. I'm a Republican."

🦌 One of the greatest exponents of Republicanism in Mitchell County was Samuel J. Turner, who represented the county in the North Carolina House of Representatives in 1887, 1895, 1909, 1919, 1920, and 1925. Although he was one of those rare persons without any sense of humor, Sam Turner was one of the most humorous of men.

Turner wrote Jeter C. Pritchard, a Republican who represented

North Carolina in the United States Senate at the turn of the century and afterward served with distinction as a United States circuit judge, asking for aid in procuring for him a lucrative position. Senator Pritchard, who was not numbered among Turner's most ardent admirers, replied, "After much effort I have secured you a job. It's cow-punching out west at five dollars a month. You'll have to furnish your own horse and saddle."

Turner was incensed by this reply. He forthwith wrote Senator Pritchard, "And, thou, Senator Pritchard sayeth unto me in substance Samuel J. Turner, thou most insignificant of mortal hinds, thrust your proboscis into the mundane earth, and root hog or die."

❦ He had a wayward son, who answered the last summons years ago. While Turner was on a journey, his wayward son begged his mother to give him the currency that she had deposited in the stocking she was wearing. She refused. The son attempted to obtain the currency by violence, and was jailed.

On returning home and learning of this sad event, Turner said to an acquaintance in his rather ponderous manner, "I never before suffered such a humiliating experience. On my return home I found my wayward son incarcerated behind prison bars, charged with attempting to feloniously extract filthy lucre from the pedal extremities of his maternal sire."

❦ Although he was licensed to practice law, Turner acquired few clients. On one of his rare appearances in the superior court of Mitchell County, he was associated in a case with two other Bakersville attorneys, Sam Black and Will Lambert. Black was compelled to absent himself from the courtroom while Lambert was addressing the jury. On his return Black asked Turner what kind of speech Lambert had made. Turner replied, "Mr. Black, it was a truly sorry performance. Indeed, it was not a whit better than yours."

❦ I note, by way of digression, that Sam Black had a waggish son who was inducted into the army in the First World War. As he was marching from Bakersville to Toe Cane with other inductees to take the train to Camp Jackson, Black's son said, "I wouldn't have to go to war if I hadn't forgotten to claim my exemption. I'm gun-shy."

❦ Avery County, which was created for the most part out of Mitchell, was established by the General Assembly in 1911. During the political campaign preceding its creation, Turner was an unsuccessful candidate for Mitchell's House seat. He appeared before the legislative committee considering the bill to establish Avery and made a vigorous speech opposing it. A staunch advocate of the bill asked him, "Didn't you tell Luther Banner at Spruce Pine during the recent campaign that you favored the establishment of the new county of Avery?"

Sam Turner responded, "I assure you, my friend, that whenever that interrogation was propounded to me during the late campaign, whether on the hustings or in private, I artfully evaded giving it an answer."

❦ During 1924 there was a bitter contest in Mitchell County among Republicans who sought their party's nomination for the county's seat in the forthcoming General Assembly. Turner was one of the contestants. Those who opposed him disseminated an accusation that while he was representing Mitchell County in 1895, he had accepted a bribe to procure the passage of a special act appointing an individual treasurer of Mitchell County. The people of Mitchell County gave no credence to the accusation. Sam Turner was nominated and elected to represent them.

After he had been seated in the House of 1925, his disgruntled foes within his own party persuaded a House committee to report a resolution directing it to investigate the accusation and to make recommendations conforming to its findings.

I was familiar with the facts. When the resolution was called up for House action, I said, "This resolution is based on a stale accusation, which had its origin in 1895—thirty years ago. During those years the courts of Mitchell County have been open, Representative Turner's disgruntled foes have not seen fit to make the accusation against him on oath to any law enforcement officer, and grand juries have met and adjourned several times annually without taking cognizance of the accusation. The accusation was noised abroad by his disgruntled foes in last year's campaign. The people of Mitchell County gave the accusation no credence. They chose Representative Turner to represent them in this House. The House ought not to waste the taxpayers' money investigating this stale accusation, or permit his disgruntled foes to wash their dirty linen in public. I move, therefore, that the resolution do lie on the table."

The House tabled the resolution. Turner repaired to my desk and said in his ponderous fashion, "Young man, you have rendered significant service to me, the House, the state, and the cause of eternal justice. My gratitude to you is unlimited, and will endure until I shuffle off my mortal coil. I pray you to call on me for any aid I can ever vouchsafe to you. I will answer your call forthwith, whether it comes to me in the burning glare of the noonday sun or in the deepest gloom of the nocturnal hour."

꙳   Willie M. Person, an attorney of Louisburg, was one of North Carolina's most flamboyant sons. He customarily wore a flaming red vest and found joy in bizarre words and deeds. During early 1929 the impending economic collapse was casting its shadows before it, and the General Assembly was finding it difficult to raise sufficient revenues to balance the state's budget.

The State Senate, of which Person was a member, reached a section of the revenue bill which contemplated the imposition of annual taxes of one dollar and two dollars on the owners of dogs and bitches, respectively. Senator Person sent forward an amendment. As a page carried the amendment to the reading clerk's desk, the senator said, "If the legislature adopts my amendment, the state's financial problems will be solved. We will not only have sufficient funds to meet all expenses, but we'll have a surplus in the treasury at the end of the biennium."

The reading clerk read Senator Person's amendment. It said, "Tax on male dogs, one dollar; tax on bitches, two dollars; tax on sons of bitches, five dollars."

꙳   On the evening before the formal opening of the General Assembly of 1931, the Democrats of the House met in caucus in the House chamber and nominated their candidates for major House offices.

After two residents of Wake County had been nominated for the post, I placed the name of a third candidate in nomination for the office of reading clerk. He was Bascom Lamar Lunsford, of Buncombe County, who in after years rightly received nationwide acclaim as one of America's foremost collectors and preservers of folk ballads and folk music.

"Fellow Democrats," I said, "we have thus far exercised political wisdom in selecting our candidates. We have chosen as our candidate for speaker, Willis Smith, an eminent resident of Wake County, which is somewhat east of the state's center. We have named as our candidate for principal clerk, Thad Eure, an able inhabitant of Gates County, which is located in the far eastern part of the state. We have selected as our candidate for engrossing clerk, Rosa Munds, a charming lady from Cabarrus County, which is situated in the state's middle section, the Piedmont. In naming our candidate for reading clerk, we must not forget the Democrats residing in the west. Like the Democrats of other areas, they are troubled by the world, the flesh, and the devil. Unlike the Democrats of many other areas, however, they are compelled to wage unceasing warfare with other foes, their Republican neighbors."

Pointing to the portrait of Zeb Vance, North Carolina's most beloved son of all time, which was hanging on the wall of the House chamber, I closed with these words: "I place in nomination as our candidate for reading clerk a Democrat who resides in Zeb Vance's great county of Buncombe, Bascom Lamar Lunsford."

Lunsford won the nomination. Next day he was elected reading clerk.

Lunsford was handicapped in the performance of his duties as reading clerk by a slight inability to pronounce correctly words unfamiliar to him. For example, he always pronounced *chiropractor* "ki-row-prax-ker."

Some of the House members, who were outstanding linguists and who esteemed the capacity to pronounce words with precision an indispensable qualification for reading clerk, became inordinately dissatisfied with Lunsford's deficiency and began to proclaim that the House had a reading clerk who could not read.

A delegation of them visited me. They said I was responsible for Lunsford being reading clerk, and they importuned me to persuade him to resign and accept another position with the House. They promised that he would be given a larger salary in the other position if he would do so.

When I communicated their wishes to him, Lunsford declared, "I was elected reading clerk, and I'm going to read."

On being thus rebuffed by Lunsford, the linguists presented to the House a resolution which asserted that the office of reading clerk was vacant and directed the House to proceed to elect an occupant for it.

When the resolution came up for House action, the linguists criticized Lunsford without mercy for his lapses in pronunciation and urged their colleagues to approve the resolution. With the endurance of a stoic, Lunsford sat in his seat in front of the speaker's dais throughout the proceedings and endured the vituperation in silence.

After the linguists had exhausted their verbal ammunition, Representatives Floyd Crouse, James L. Gwaltney, Jack Morphew, and I took up the cudgels in Lunsford's behalf.

All of us used humor as weapons except Representative Gwaltney, who made an emotional speech in which he charged that the linguists had visited foul insults on all those legislators who, like himself, had not been taught the niceties of pronunciation.

Jack Morphew gave the House this warning: "There are far more serious deficiencies in public officials than calling chiropractor 'ki-row-prax-ker.' I warn you against declaring public offices vacant because their occupants are incompetent to fill them. If such a rule were adopted and applied to the members of this House, I would certainly be expelled from this chamber. But I would be closely followed by many others, including some who can pronounce chiropractor with precise exactness."

One of the representatives most distressed by Lunsford's inadequacy was Union L. Spence, a perfectionist of Moore County, who was chairman of the Committee on Finance and one of the House's ablest members. He was the only member of the House who pronounced the word *finance* as "fin-nance." Representative Spence had made a somewhat bitter speech in favor of the resolution.

When I spoke, I told the House I opposed the resolution for two reasons. In the first place, I said, the resolution alleges that the office of reading clerk is vacant. Pointing to Lunsford, I added, "That allegation is false. We have a reading clerk. He is sitting in his seat in front of the speaker's dais ready to perform his duty and read this resolution to the House just as soon as the talking stops.

"My second reason for opposing the resolution arises out of my concern for my beloved friend, the gentleman from Moore. If the seats of all those in this chamber who pronounce 'fin-nance' as if it were 'fi-nance' should be declared to be vacant, all of the legislative burdens of the House would fall upon the gentleman from Moore. Although his shoulders are broad and strong, I do not believe he ought to be compelled to carry such heavy burdens alone."

When the battle ended, the House overwhelmingly defeated the resolution and retained the reading clerk who allegedly could not read. Lunsford ameliorated the grief of the linguists somewhat in future days by permitting his assistant, Phil Whitley, to read to the House the most complicated bills and resolutions.

~ The General Assembly of 1931 met in the depth of the Great Depression and had the unhappy task of finding ways and means to keep the schools of the state open and to enable the state to discharge its other essential functions. Inspired by its own devotion and courageous Governor O. Max Gardner, the General Assembly performed its task well, although its performance required its members to remain in Raleigh at their own expense many days beyond the sixty days for which they received a meager recompense.

During these trying times, Representative Joe Garibaldi, a beloved member from Mecklenburg who was affectionately called Uncle Joe by his colleagues, enlivened many otherwise dark moments in the House with his quiet and recurring wit. I cite an example.

Representative Albert E. White, a banker of Robeson County, explained to the House a local bill which he had introduced. In doing so, he emulated the cautious banker who presented to his board of directors in neutral fashion the application of a friend for an unsecured loan when he was torn between a wish for his friend to obtain the loan and a fear that his friend might be insolvent.

When Representative White sat down, Uncle Joe arose and said, "Mr. Speaker, I want to vote on my good friend's local bill in accordance with his wishes. To do this, I must put to him this question: Are you fur your bill or agin it?"

Apart from the hypocrisy that prompted some of them to vote for the Turlington Act, my colleagues in the three assemblies in which I served were stalwart North Carolinians who practiced with fidelity Grover Cleveland's aphorism "A public office is a public trust" and sought to attune their official actions with the best interests of the state they loved.

℞   Representative Loomis F. Kluttz, a Catawba County attorney, had been one of the advocates of the Poole bill as his county's representative in the House of 1925. When he sought reelection to the House in the ensuing election, he made prohibition and opposition to evolution the major planks in his platform. His Democratic opponent was Gus Self, a brilliant and courageous attorney of Hickory.

They met in debate at Conover. Loomis had been a student at the Emerson College of Oratory in Boston and was a florid public speaker. When he and Gus met in debate at Conover, Loomis spoke first.

He made two accusations against Gus. They were that Gus, who was an avowed opponent of sumptuary laws, wanted to go to the legislature to repeal the Volstead Act and that he would vote against any law outlawing the teaching of evolution if he were elected.

In elaborating what he said about evolution, Loomis said, "Those who preach and teach evolution are the agents of the devil. They are trying to destroy the Christian truth that God created the universe and man. They maintain that everything was created by some strange evolutionary process and not by God, and that all men are descended from monkeys. If you elect me to the legislature, I'll have a law passed outlawing the teaching of the diabolical theory of evolution in North Carolina's schools forever."

Gus loathed hypocrisy and loved truth. In replying to Loomis, he admitted he thought the Volstead Act ought to be repealed. He added, however, that he was not seeking election to the North Carolina House to secure the repeal of the Volstead Act, because the act was a federal and not a state law.

He also frankly admitted that he was opposed to all legislative attempts to set limits on human thought on any subject, and for that reason would vote against any proposal to prohibit the teaching of evolution in state institutions of learning in case he should be elected to the legislature.

He asserted he believed all human beings to be the children of God, and he knew little about evolution, although he cherished the hope that mankind was advancing with the processes of the sun.

In ending his reply on the subject of evolution, Gus said, "I don't know whether or not evolutionists believe that men are descended from monkeys, and I don't care. Having known Loomis Kluttz's father, who was a fine old country doctor at Maiden, however, I do know one thing with certainty. Sometimes a monkey is descended from a man, and Loomis Kluttz constitutes conclusive proof of that fact."

In combination, Republicans and fundamentalists defeated loyal Democrats, and Loomis Kluttz was reelected Catawba's representative.

~   State Senator George Penny, of Greensboro, was a highly skilled auctioneer whose services were in constant demand. Having contracted to auction lots in a new residential development in a New England town, he traveled to the town several days before the auction was to be held.

On arising late on the morning of July Fourth, George saw nobody except the lone waiter who served him breakfast at the hotel where he was a guest and the hotel room clerk. On inquiring of the clerk, George learned that the inhabitants of the community esteemed the nation's natal day to be the most important day of the year. They always celebrated it in appropriate fashion, and virtually all of them were then gathered at an open-air platform just beyond the crest of a nearby hill to hear two of the town's most respected citizens discuss the identity of the Americans who had served the country best.

George joined the gathering at the platform. He observed two elderly gentlemen seated on the platform, one a short, fat man and the other a tall, skinny man. The tall, skinny man was accompanied by his old-maid daughter, a teacher of history in the local school, for the purpose, George was soon told, to forestall the known forgetfulness of the father.

The master of ceremonies presented the short, fat man as the first speaker. When he arose, he declared that a great New Englander, Daniel Webster, was the greatest of all America's great sons. He extolled Webster's services to the nation without stint.

As he proceeded, the increasing ruddiness of the face of the tall, skinny man revealed his mounting anger. When he arose to reply, he snorted, "It is absurd to maintain that Daniel Webster was the greatest of all Americans. The greatest of all Americans was Old Hickory Jackson, who led our army to victory at the Battle of New Orleans. And where was Daniel Webster, I ask my friend, when Old Hickory was exposing his breast to the bullets of the enemy at New Orleans. He was in a bomb-proof shelter at Boston writing a dictionary."

The daughter pulled her father's coattails and said, "Father, that wasn't Daniel; that was Noah."

The old man roared, "Noah, hell! Noah didn't write a dictionary. He built the ark."

Chapter 10

Humor in
Congress

ए ए ए

My younger brother, Joseph Wilson Ervin, a lawyer of
Charlotte, died on Christmas Day, 1945, while representing the old Ninth District in the Seventy-ninth
Congress. Pursuant to law, the Democratic congressional committee
of the district met in Newton to nominate a Democratic candidate
for the remainder of the term.

After many ballots the committee was unable to agree on a nominee. Joe L. Blythe, of Charlotte, the chairman of the committee,
called me and told me, "We're hopelessly deadlocked on those whose
names have been placed in nomination. We've caucused privately
and found that we can nominate you unanimously. Will you accept
our nomination?"

"Joe, I've never had any ambition to serve in Congress," I replied.
"But if the committee will nominate me on the condition that I will
not run for reelection, I'll help the committee out of its dilemma by
accepting the nomination."

I was elected to the Seventy-ninth Congress without opposition in
the special election on January 25, 1946, and served in the House
for approximately a year. Despite urging from some constituents to
the contrary, I declined to seek reelection and resumed the practice
of law.

On motion of "Farmer Bob" Doughton, the dean of the North
Carolina delegation, Speaker Sam Rayburn administered the oath
of office to me, and I was assigned to membership on the Post Office
and Post Roads Committee, which was headed by a fine Virginian,
Thomas G. Burch.

The other representatives from North Carolina at that time were

Graham A. Barden, Herbert C. Bonner, Alfred L. Bulwinkle, William Olin Burgin, Bayard Clark, Harold D. Cooley, Carl T. Durham, John H. Folger, John H. Kerr, and Zebulon Weaver. Burgin died in office, and Jane Pratt, the only woman ever elected to Congress from North Carolina, was named to succeed him in a special election.

The Second World War had ended on August 14, 1945, with the surrender of the Japanese. Inasmuch as the laws establishing the draft and the Office of Price Administration (OPA) were expiring, the Congress had to determine what action it should take in respect to them.

The committees on Military and Naval Affairs presented to the House a bill to continue the draft on these conditions: first, nobody was to be drafted before his majority; second, nobody was to be drafted before a specified date in the future; and, third, nobody was to be drafted on the specified date unless the president determined that the national defense so required.

The bill did not illustrate the grandest moment of legislative valor. The date on which it was to take effect, if ever, was after the next election, and the circumstance that all of America's youth of eighteen years and upward had already been called for service in the armed forces was ignored by it.

I borrowed two and a half minutes of the time allotted to the Democrats and two minutes of the time allotted to the Republicans for debate on the bill, and joined two stalwart representatives, James W. Wadsworth, of New York, and Ewing Thomason, of Texas, in denouncing the bill as a draft law under which nobody could be drafted. Incidentally, this was the longest speech I was ever permitted to make to the House.

After its passage by the House, the bill was much improved in the Senate.

❧   Congress also passed an act extending the life of OPA. President Harry S. Truman deemed the act ineffective, vetoed it, and appealed to the nation to call on Congress to enact an adequate law on the subject.

In response to this appeal, I received from constituents what I thought at the time was an avalanche of letters—about two hundred. Some of the writers were producers who demanded the removal of all price controls, and others were consumers who insisted that price controls should be retained.

The most intriguing of the letters was one from a small businessman in Charlotte, who proposed a formula for governmental price fixing which would have been pleasing to all if anyone had been smart enough to devise procedures to make it operative. He suggested that Congress ought to remove price ceilings from the things he sold and keep them on the things he bought.

As head of the OPA, Chester Bowles sometimes moved in mysterious ways his wonders to perform. For example, he refused to authorize the manufacturers of ordinary dress shirts to raise their prices trifling amounts to keep their manufacture profitable, but permitted them to use the same or a lesser amount of material to make fantastic sport shirts, which they were allowed to sell for exorbitant prices. As a result, ordinary dress shirts virtually disappeared from the market, and fantastic sport shirts proliferated.

Inasmuch as I had practically worn out my supply of ordinary dress shirts, I visited one Washington haberdashery after another searching for replacements. I could find none. I noted, however, that haberdashery shelves were piled to the ceiling with sport shirts unsuitable for everyday wear.

About this time I received an invitation from a committee to attend at my own expense a banquet it was giving to honor Chester Bowles for his outstanding accomplishments as head of OPA. I yielded to the temptation to notify the committee I could not accept its invitation because I "didn't have a wearable shirt."

❦ In describing events that occurred on the floor of the House or the Senate, I paraphrase what was said by the participants instead of attempting to quote what they said verbatim. If I quoted with exactness what they said, readers would find scant corroboration of it in the permanent edition of the *Congressional Record*. This is true for two reasons.

Representatives and senators often modify or even eliminate their original remarks for the permanent edition of the *Record* either to protect their own political flanks or to avoid offense to colleagues.

As my good friend Senator Paul Douglas, of Illinois, was wont to say, every speaker has three speeches: the one he intends to make, the one he actually makes, and the one he wished he had made. By permitting a representative or senator to revise his remarks as originally transcribed for its permanent edition, the *Congressional Record* enables him to make the speech he wished he had made. These considerations engender my belief that in spots the permanent edition of the *Record* is more of a work of fiction than one of fact.

❦　Representative Frank E. Hook, of Michigan, was a pronounced liberal in the modern acceptation of that much abused term. He had a propensity for declaring with fervid eloquence on the House floor that human rights are superior to property rights.

An old conservative Republican, whose name has escaped my memory, interrupted Representative Hook while he was speaking on the superiority of human rights over property rights and said, "Mr. Speaker, some of us think that property rights are simply rights belonging to human beings, and want the distinguished gentleman from Michigan to explain to us what he thinks is the distinction between the rights he calls human rights and property rights. If he will yield to me for the purpose, I'd like to state to him a premise and put to him a question based on it."

Representative Hook graciously yielded, and the old conservative Republican stated his premise and question in this way: "In early days, the frontiersman invaded the wilderness with his axe in one hand and his rifle in the other. With his axe, he felled trees, hewed them into logs, and built a log cabin to shelter his family. My question is this, Was the frontiersman's undoubted right to occupy the cabin his hands had erected a human right or a property right?"

Although he ordinarily had answers for all questions, Representative Hook meekly replied, "I don't know."

❦　Frank B. Keefe, a Republican representative from Wisconsin, was not overly fond of any Democrats. His pet abomination, however, was a recently elected and very liberal young Democratic representative from his own state.

The House had under consideration a resolution which allocated an additional appropriation of fifty thousand dollars to the House

Un-American Activities Committee to enable it to continue its investigation of Communism. At that time this committee was the favorite target of the most pronounced liberals. The young Democrat from Wisconsin made a speech in opposition to the resolution.

On the demand of its proponents, a roll-call vote on the resolution was ordered. I do not suggest that the young Democrat changed his mind because of any apprehension that he and Vito Marcantonio, a representative from New York who was reputed to be a Communist, might be the only members of the House recorded against the resolution when the roll was called. On the contrary, I am sure his change of mind was motivated solely by his patriotism. When the roll was called, the young Democrat joined virtually all other representatives in voting for the resolution.

As Alben W. Barkley was wont to say, a representative or a senator heaps encomiums on a colleague just before he sticks a stiletto in his back.

Frank Keefe arose and said, "Mr. Speaker, in my advancing years I am getting hard of hearing. I could not hear how my distinguished, eminent, illustrious, and wise young colleague from Wisconsin voted on the resolution."

Speaker Sam Rayburn said, "He is recorded as having voted for the resolution."

Frank Keefe remarked, "Evidently, Mr. Speaker, the speech which my distinguished, eminent, illustrious, and wise young colleague from Wisconsin made against the resolution was no more convincing to him than it was to the intelligent members of the House."

❧ My next-door neighbor in the House Office Building was Charles M. LaFollette, a Republican representative from Evansville, Indiana, who entertained extremely liberal views. He was not overly fond of orthodox Republicans, and Southern Democrats were anathema to him.

LaFollette entered the contest for the Republican nomination for United States senator in Indiana, where the nomination was to be made in convention and the statewide Republican leaders were reputed to be rather mossback. In his quest for the nomination, he spoke throughout Indiana, expressing the liberal views he entertained. These views proved to be heresy to the delegates to the convention, and they overwhelmingly rejected his bid for the senatorial nomination.

Immediately after his defeat, LaFollette issued a statement to the press in which he said, in essence, "I've decided that the Republican party is not the vehicle for obtaining progressive legislation. Consequently, I'm going to sever my connection with it on the expiration of my term in Congress. But I don't want anybody to think I'm going to join the Democrats. I couldn't be a Democrat unless and until the Democrats get rid of their southern appendage." That was his favorite term for Southern Democrats.

On the following morning, LaFollette was in his seat in the House. John Rankin, the sometimes obstreperous and always entertaining representative from Tupelo, Mississippi, arose and read the statement that LaFollette had issued to the press. He then added: "Representative LaFollette's statement to the effect that he is leaving the Republicans, but is not joining the Democrats, reminds me of an old friend of mine who loves to browse in old cemeteries in Mississippi and read the epitaphs on the gravestones. He always carries a pocketful of chalk with him and rubs it on indistinct epitaphs to make their words legible. One day my friend discovered this epitaph on a gravestone:

> Pause thou stranger, passing by,
> As you are now, so once was I;
> As I am now, you soon will be;
> Prepare for death, and follow me.

"When my friend read that epitaph, he felt like I did when I read Representative LaFollette's statement. He pulled out a piece of chalk from his pocket and wrote these words under it:

> To follow you I'll not consent,
> Until I know which way you went."

Chapter 11

Humor
in the
North Carolina
Supreme Court

ॐ ॐ ॐ

Humor has not been lacking in the North Carolina Supreme Court.

Major Quincy F. Neal, who was a lawyer in mountainous Ashe County and better known for his frankness than for his legal erudition, argued an appeal before the North Carolina Supreme Court at a time when its presiding officer was Chief Justice William N. H. Smith, who was deeply versed in the niceties of the law and somewhat impatient with those who were less erudite than he. Major Neal was expounding to the court the simplest propositions of law. Chief Justice Smith interrupted him with this inquiry: "Major, can't you assume that this court knows the elementary principles of law?" The major responded, "Your Honor, I assumed that the last time I was before this court, and I lost my case."

ॐ The court's most resourceful humorist was Justice Willis J. Brogden. In explaining the toll that those who control the destinies of the court charge its members, he said, "They put you in a mausoleum while you are living and hang you in effigy after you have gone."

Humor often crept into his opinions. In writing an opinion setting aside a judgment in favor of a plaintiff injured by the defendant's mule, Justice Brogden said, "A mule is a melancholy creature. It is *nullius filius* in the animal kingdom. It has been said that a mule has neither 'pride of ancestry nor hope of posterity.' Josh Billings has remarked that if he had to preach the funeral of a mule, he would stand at its head. Men love and pet horses, dogs, cats, and lambs. Nobody loves or pets a mule. No poet has ever penned a sonnet or an ode to him, and no prose writer has ever paid a tribute to his good qualities. . . . The idealist may dream of the day 'when the world is safe for democracy,' but this event will perhaps arrive long before the world will be safe from the heels of a mule."

❦   A plaintiff habitually bought the lands of others at tax foreclosure sales and habitually failed in his efforts to procure valid deeds for the land he purchased. In affirming a judgment holding one of the deeds invalid, Justice Brogden said, "The plaintiff in his brief says: 'When the rich young ruler went to Christ and asked what should he do to inherit eternal life, the Great Teacher told him how he could do so, and the young ruler told Christ that he had done all the things enumerated, and asked the Master, "What lackest I now?" and the Great Teacher told him what he should do in addition to what he had done. I most respectfully contend that I have done what is laid down in the statutes in cases of this kind, and I most respectfully ask this court, "What lackest I now?"' In the first place, the plaintiff 'lacks' an accurate reference to the rich young ruler, as will appear from an examination of the record, Mark 10:17–23, Luke 18:18–23. The biblical record discloses that the rich young ruler lacked only one thing; while, on the other hand, the title of plaintiff lacks several essentials to a valid tax title."

❦   On another occasion, the same plaintiff appealed to the Supreme Court from an adverse ruling in respect to one of his tax deeds. In writing an opinion upholding the ruling, Justice Brogden said, "Plaintiff in his brief says: 'I take much pleasure in informing this court that I have read every one of your reports from vol. 140 to 193, inclusive, and with the hundreds of opinions, I have found nothing that in law would support the judgment sent up in the record.' In view of the fact that the uniform holding of the court supports the judgment rendered, the plaintiff's aforesaid declaration in the brief calls to mind the colloquy between Philip and a notable citizen of Ethiopia, occurring long ago. The distinguished citizen of

Ethiopia was undertaking to read the Book of the Law, and the great evangelist propounded to him this query: 'Understandest thou what thou readest?' Acts 8:30."

꙳ In another case the accused was convicted by the jury of murder in the second degree. On his appeal he contended that the evidence offered by the prosecution, which was wholly circumstantial, was insufficient to sustain the verdict and that the trial court erred in denying his motion for nonsuit. After detailing in minute detail the multitude of circumstances invoked by the prosecution and admitting that, "standing alone," some of "this evidence was slight," the majority of the court adjudged that, in combination, the circumstances were sufficient to carry the case to the jury and warrant the verdict.

Justice Brogden wrote a dissenting opinion which challenged in devastating fashion the probative value of the circumstantial evidence. In closing his dissent, he said, "I do not know whether or not the defendant is guilty. All I know is the record which I have before me. From this record the deceased was associating with other men, and the evidence does not point 'unerringly to the defendant's guilt,' nor does it create more than a suspicion or possibility of the guilt of the defendant. The record leaves upon my mind the impression that the horror of the crime demanded a victim, and that as a result thereof the defendant was bound as a smoking sacrifice upon the altar of conjecture and suspicion. . . . It is contended that the facts and circumstances are so slight in probative value that in themselves and standing alone they would not amount to evidence, but when taken in combination they constitute a rope of great strength. I do not concur in this reasoning. Unless the principles of mathematics have been recently changed, adding a column of zeros together produces zero; neither can a multitude of legal zeros beget a legal entity."

꙳ Justice Brogden endeared himself to the North Carolina bar by his humor, by his legal learning, and by a habit to which few appellate judges are addicted. He listened with rapt attention to the oral arguments of attorneys and refrained from interrupting them with questions. He was wont to say that most of the attorneys who argued appeals had prepared the cases thoroughly and would make their positions understandable to the court with more dispatch if they were allowed to proceed in their own way.

At that time the state statute empowered the governor to call special terms of the superior court, to commission the judges to hold them, and to order the calling of grand jurors in case they were for the trial of criminal actions.

Harry Baxter, who was represented by Judge Walter D. Siler, had been tried for murder in the first degree before Victor Maurice Barnhill, then a superior court judge, and a jury at a special term of the superior court of Chatham County upon an indictment returned by the grand jury. The petit jury found Baxter guilty of murder in the first degree, and Judge Barnhill entered a judgment that he suffer death.

The record on Baxter's appeal disclosed no authority for the holding of the special term at which he was indicted and convicted except a carbon copy of a letter from the executive clerk in the governor's office advising the chairman of the Board of Commissioners of Chatham County that he had called the special term and assigned Judge Barnhill to hold it. No order calling the special term, no commission assigning Judge Barnhill to hold it, and no order calling grand jurors appeared in the record, or could be found.

Judge Siler contended that the indictment under which Baxter had been tried and convicted was void because it had been returned by a grand jury without lawful authority, and that for this reason judgment of death on his conviction of the crime charged in the indictment should be arrested by the Supreme Court. In his oral argument, Siler said, "This is the situation as the law must view it. A fellow named Barnhill, who had nothing else to do, drove to the Chatham County Courthouse in Pittsboro. He went to the sheriff's office and asked him if there was anybody in jail who ought to be tried. The sheriff said, 'Yes. Baxter.' Barnhill instructed the sheriff to bring in a bunch of fellows to indict and try Baxter. The sheriff obeyed. An illegal indictment was returned by an illegal grand jury, an illegal verdict was returned by an illegal petit jury, and an illegal death sentence was pronounced by a judge acting illegally."

For the only time during his service on the bench, Judge Brogden interrupted the argument of an advocate with a question. He asked, "Judge Siler, wasn't anything done in accordance with the law?"

Judge Siler paused for a second, and then replied, "Yes, Your Honor. They rang the courthouse bell."

The Supreme Court arrested the judgment and ordered Baxter's case tried anew.

Furnifold M. Simmons, who had served with much ability as a United States senator from North Carolina since 1901, bolted the national Democratic ticket in 1928 and supported Herbert Hoover for president. As the North Carolina Democratic primary neared in 1930, multitudes of Democrats urged Justice Brogden to seek nomination in opposition to Senator Simmons. He declined, and Josiah W. Bailey became the nominee.

A few days later I met Justice Brogden in Chapel Hill and said to him, "Like thousands of other Tar Heels, I thought you would make an outstanding senator and regretted you did not seek the nomination."

Justice Brogden responded, "I knew I was not financially able to defray the cost of a Senate campaign myself, and that I would have to depend on others to do that if I ran. I'm accustomed to having mortgages on my property, but I don't want other people to feel that they might have a mortgage on me."

Robert Gregg Cherry, who was known as Gregg, and I served in the North Carolina House of Representatives in 1931. Afterwards he tried numerous cases before me when I presided in the superior court of his home county of Gaston.

In late January, 1948, Governor Gregg Cherry called me, told me that North Carolina Supreme Court Justice Michael Schenck had retired a few minutes before because of ill health, and offered me an immediate appointment to the Supreme Court as his successor. Inasmuch as this was a bolt out of the blue to me, I asked the governor to let me consider the matter until the next day, and he acceded to my request.

I lay awake all night, torn between my ambition to serve on the

Supreme Court and my realizations that I still owed debts incurred during the Great Depression, that I had three children to educate, and that my income as a practicing lawyer was about three times the emoluments of a state Supreme Court justice.

On the following morning I informed Governor Cherry I had decided to decline the high honor he had tendered me.

Soon thereafter, Fred S. Hutchins, a longtime friend in Winston-Salem, called me and told me that the Forsyth County bar had endorsed me that morning for the vacancy caused by Justice Schenck's retirement. As its representative, he had advised Governor Cherry that I was its choice for the vacancy and had learned that I was also the governor's choice but that I had declined the post. The governor had told Fred that he would be pleased if Fred could persuade me to change my mind.

Fred did, and on February 3, 1948, I became a member of the court. I served until June 11, 1954, when I resigned and qualified as a member of the United States Senate. Meanwhile, I had been nominated without opposition and elected without difficulty to the remainder of Justice Schenck's term and a regular term of eight years.

After I took my oath of office as a Supreme Court justice, I was seated on the bench in the extreme left seat assigned to the junior member, and my right-hand colleague, Justice Seawell, whispered to me, "You've got the best seat on the court. You can look out the window and watch the squirrels running up and down the trees on the capitol grounds and ignore the nuts who argue cases before us."

❧   At that time, the court consisted of Chief Justice Walter P. Stacy, and associate justices William Augustus Devin, Maurice Victor Barnhill, John Wallace Winborne, Aaron Ashley Flowers Seawell, Emery Byrd Denny, and me.

Chief Justice Stacy died September 13, 1951, and Justice Devin succeeded him as chief justice. Itimous T. Valentine and Robert Hunt Parker served successively in the associate justiceship vacated by Devin. Justice Seawell died October 14, 1950, and Murray G. James and Jefferson D. Johnson, Jr., successively filled the vacancy caused by his death. Devin retired as chief in 1954, and was succeeded by Justice Barnhill, whose replacement as associate justice was William H. Bobbitt.

When I attended my first Supreme Court conference, Chief Justice Stacy advised me that all votes were taken in the inverse order of seniority to remove the possibility that junior justices might be influenced unduly by their seniors, and that in consequence I should not only vote first as to how cases should be decided but should state the reasons for my votes. He added, "Good ideas are helpful, and the best way to destroy bad ideas is to expose them and let others swat them."

Unlike most appellate courts, the justices selected in rotation the cases in which they wished to write opinions. I found the other justices to be most congenial and cooperative co-laborers in the judicial vineyard. All of them except Chief Justice Stacy, who was a widower, had charming wives, who afforded my wife delightful companionship.

Although he seemed oblivious to her existence, Chief Justice Stacy was loved from afar by a lady who never neglected an opportunity to ask his associates and their wives with deep solicitude and in whispers as to how he was. Justice Denny dubbed her "Whispering Hope."

My wife and I treasure our associations with the justices and their wives among our most joyous recollections.

❧   As a practicing lawyer, I had often read the opinions of appellate courts which reminded me of the story of a little church in the boondocks.

The church had fired its preacher, who insisted that the chairman of the board of deacons should reveal to him the reasons for the church's action. The preacher asked the chairman, "Didn't I argufy?" The chairman answered, "You sure did argufy." The preacher inquired, "Didn't I sputify?" The chairman responded, "You sure did sputify." "Then why did the congregation fire me?" the preacher demanded. The chairman replied, "You didn't show wherein."

I have read many judicial opinions that disclosed what the court decided, but did not really reveal how or why it reached its decision. When I assumed my seat on the North Carolina Supreme Court, I did so with the determination to write my opinions in plain English which requires neither explanation nor interpretation.

Some judges, legislators, and writers of regulations ignore the truth that men invented language to communicate their ideas to each other. It is a symptom of judicial laziness or inordinate erudition for a judge to couch his opinions in words that conceal rather than reveal what he says. Americans are the most law- and regulation-ridden people on earth. The fact that their government issues its manifold edicts in ambiguous language whose meaning is elusive to the most sophisticated lawyers and linguists only adds to their plight. The chief offender is the *Federal Register*, which publishes each year thousands of pages of federal regulations in virtually incomprehensible gobbledegook. An ironic act of Congress makes all human beings in our land, no matter how illiterate or uneducated they may be, legally responsible for comprehending completely the meaning of every word in the *Federal Register*.

Judges, lawyers, law teachers, law students, and others have graciously assured me that I did write my opinions as a Supreme Court justice with unmistakable clarity. One of the judges paid me the tribute of saying that a person did not need to be a lawyer to understand my opinions.

❧   I am constrained to admit, however, that I fell far short of my goal in one of my earlier opinions. The case in which it was written involved a perplexing legal question. My diligent search for authorities in all jurisdictions did not disclose any helpful precedents.

By agonizing mental turmoil, I produced an opinion. My brethren approved it, and it became the opinion of the court. After it was published in the court's advance sheets, I received a letter from David H. Henderson, now an eminent member of the Charlotte bar, who was then a student in the Duke University Law School. Dave wrote, "I don't understand your opinion in that case. Please explain it to me." Candor compelled me to send him this reply: "I'm sorry I can't explain my opinion to you. I don't understand it myself."

❧   A young lawyer was making his first oral argument, which he had obviously memorized, before the court. Chief Justice Stacy, who hid his kind heart behind a serious face, picked up a short pencil, pointed it at the young man, and asked him a question about the case. The lawyer lost his composure, confessed he could not answer the chief justice's question, and floundered badly.

Being desirous of rehabilitating him, I said, "Although we wear black robes, we are very compassionate. Forget you are standing before the bench, imagine that you have just met me on Fayetteville Street, and tell me in your own way what the case is about."

My remarks had a miraculous effect on the young lawyer. He recovered his composure, ignored what he had memorized, argued the case with clarity, and won it.

Conferences were sometimes intriguing. The justices often argued among themselves over cases with more vigor than the attorneys had displayed in their oral arguments. At other times the justices bantered each other. In *Hubbard* versus *Wiggins*, the court was required to interpret the will of an old lady whose nouns and verbs, like Maude Muller's, did not agree, and whose portfolio contained six United States Savings Bonds which were bequeathable by her and three United States Savings Bonds which were not.

While the ambiguous will raised a number of questions, the substantial one presented was whether the words "Sam Hubbard is to have the bonds and one hundred dollars" bequeathed to her nephew Sam Hubbard the six bonds or the three bonds. My college-mate and longtime friend Justice Denny had prepared a proposed ruling that the testatrix had left her nephew the three bonds that the law disabled her to will, and I had prepared a proposed counterruling that the testatrix had left her nephew the six bonds that the law authorized her to will.

By a 4-to-3 vote the justices approved Justice Denny's proposed ruling and rejected mine. By this action, Justice Denny's ruling became the majority opinion and mine the minority.

After the vote, I told Justice Denny, "That's a good will you've written for the old lady. But it's your will, and not hers. As soon as the conference adjourns, I'm going to tack a sign on your office door, saying, 'Post mortem wills a specialty.'"

Justice Denny referred to a recent case in which I had done judicial patchwork on an ambiguous amendment to the state Workmen's Compensation Act and thereby converted it into a fairly presentable legislative enactment. He warned me that if I tacked the sign on his office door, he would retaliate by tacking one on my office door proclaiming, "Legislative repair shop open for business."

❧ I wrote an opinion for the court in *State* versus *Jim Palmer* which adjudged that the testimony for the prosecution was totally lacking in probative value, and that in consequence the black defendant, who had been convicted of murder in the first degree and sentenced to death, was entitled to his immediate release from death row in the state's prison where he had been confined since his trial.

A reporter forthwith visited Palmer, informed him of the Supreme Court's decision, and asked him how it felt to get off death row. Palmer made this philosophical reply to the reporter: "Boss, we never get off death's row. We're on death's row from the day we are born until the day we die."

❧ I also wrote an opinion for the court in *Brown* versus *Estates Corporation*. My opinion ended with these words: "This brings us to the appeal of the defendants, which challenges the validity of the portion of the order allowing the plaintiff's 'thirty days to amend and/or make new parties.' The presiding judge murdered the King's, the Queen's, and everybody's English by using the monstrous linguistic abomination 'and/or' in this portion of the order. We are constrained to adjudge, however, that the judge's law is better than his grammar, and that this portion of the order finds sanction in G.S. 1-163, which vests in the judge of the Superior Court discretionary authority to permit an amendment 'when the amendment does not change substantially the claim or defense.'"

One of the first congratulatory notes received by me after my appointment to the Senate was from Henry A. McKinnon, of Lumberton, who addressed it to "Judge and/or Senator Ervin."

Chapter 12

Humor in the Senate

ʝ ʝ ʝ

On May 12, 1954, Senator Clyde R. Hoey, a truly great human being, quietly died sitting in a Senate chair in front of the desk on which I scribble these words. Governor William B. Umstead was empowered to name somebody to occupy the Senate seat that his death had made vacant until the general election in November.

I had held Bill Umstead in high admiration and deep affection ever since a far-off day in September, 1913, when I, a bashful freshman, attended a Bible class which he, a sophomore, taught each Sunday morning in his room in the Old East dormitory at Chapel Hill. As the class neared its end, Bill unexpectedly asked me to lead in prayer. I stammered out, "Lord, help us. Amen." After class, I told Bill I was not accustomed to pray in public and requested him not to embarrass me by calling on me again. Bill, who had a delightful sense of humor, responded, "I've heard preachers pray for hours about our needs. You covered them fully in less than half a dozen words."

Governor Umstead was always a deliberative official; he welcomed advice from those he respected, but always made his own decision in the end. His customary deliberativeness was lengthened at that time by a serious heart attack which he had suffered soon after his inauguration and which had slowed him down substantially.

For days after the Senate vacancy arose, Governor Umstead received recommendations from various delegations and individuals concerning whom he should appoint to succeed Senator Hoey. I suggested former governor Gregg Cherry. Although I was not an aspirant, I was often mentioned in the press as one of the scores of persons being considered by the governor. Whenever anyone mentioned that fact, I habitually rejoined that being mentioned as a possible appointee to the Senate reminded me of what Mark Twain said when he was awarded the French Legion of Honor: "It's an honor few managed to escape."

Since the state Supreme Court had completed all spring term hearings, it had been recessed to enable the justices to finish their last opinions and a final conference had been scheduled prior to summer adjournment. I returned to Raleigh from a visit to Morganton to attend the conference. After its conclusion, I went to Chief Justice Barnhill's office at his request. The chief justice advised me that Governor Umstead wanted to talk to me. He added, "I don't know what the governor wants to talk to you about, but I suspect it's the Senate appointment. Although we don't want to lose you on the court, I urge you to accept the appointment if he offers it to you. The situation in Washington is deplorable."

I called the governor, who asked me to visit him at the Governor's Mansion that afternoon. Governor Umstead and I met on a secluded side porch at the mansion. After we had reminisced respecting old times, the governor said, "I'm much concerned with the Senate appointment. As a result of my service in the House and Senate, I am much troubled by the fact that so many of those in high places in Washington put far more value on political expediency than they do on fundamentals. I want to name someone to the Senate who can remain in it a long time, and acquire seniority and influence. I'm not offering you the appointment. I merely wish to determine whether you would accept it if I tendered it."

"I sincerely hope you will not offer it to me," I responded. "Despite my political activity of the past, my first love is law, not politics. I wish to stay in the administration of justice, either as a judge or as a trial lawyer. Despite my personal wishes, however, I would accept appointment to the Senate as a duty if you were to offer it to me."

Governor Umstead continued, "Although some individuals have urged me to name you, all of the organized delegations visiting me have recommended others. Soon after they started coming, I adopted the practice of stating other names to them and asking them, 'If I don't appoint your man, which of these would you like for me to appoint?' In virtually every instance, they said you were their second choice. Since my attack, my former law partner and your loyal friend, Percy Reade, of Durham, has been coming by occasionally and taking me to ride in his car. Soon after Clyde Hoey died, Percy urged me strongly to appoint you at once. He came by yesterday afternoon. When I told him the Senate appointment was giving me much concern, Percy said, 'If you'd take my advice, you'd name Sam Ervin and spend your time worrying about other things.'

"I want you to promise me one thing if I should name you senator, and that is that you will seek reelection. I won't ask you how you will vote as a senator. I am familiar with your philosophy of government, and know it will keep you straight."

As he bade me goodbye, Governor Umstead said, "Remember, I haven't promised to appoint you senator. I may never appoint you, or I may appoint you tomorrow." I responded, "Remember, I surely hope you will not offer the appointment to me."

The next morning Governor Umstead appointed me to succeed Hoey as senator from North Carolina. I took my oath of office before Vice-President Richard M. Nixon at noon, June 11, 1954. I was reelected to the Senate by my constituents in subsequent elections and served in it until December 31, 1974, when I voluntarily retired.

ξ During my days in politics, I refrained from saying unkind things about opposing candidates. In fact, I ignored their candidacies. During the campaign of 1962, the Republican nominee sought to embroil me in controversy by sending me multitudes of politically motivated telegrams demanding that I reveal at once my positions on multitudinous issues. He habitually issued copies of the telegrams to the press, and I habitually ignored them.

I could not ignore one of them, however, because it reached my office during my absence, and my secretary telegraphed my opponent that I would answer him on my return. At that time I wired my opponent as follows: "Your telegram requires no answer. My position on all issues you mention is well known to all intelligent and informed North Carolinians."

My Republican opponent in 1968 sought to secure publicity for his campaign and draw me out by issuing to the press statements making various charges against me. I ignored what he said.

A few days before the election I met a near neighbor of his at a

Democratic rally, and his neighbor told me, "Yesterday I asked your opponent how his campaign is going. He replied, 'I'm laboring under serious handicaps. Senator Ervin ignores the charges I make against him, and is giving the people the impression that he is running without opposition.'"

❦ Shortly after I entered the Senate, I initiated a weekly radio program under the guidance of my aide, Harry Gatton, to keep North Carolinians informed as to my official activities. Soon thereafter an amusing event occurred.

Although I had made live radio broadcasts, I had never heard my recorded voice on radio. As Harry and I were traveling by car to North Carolina, Harry turned on the car radio, and I heard a speaker describing the salient features of a revenue bill which was then being considered by the Senate. I said, "Harry, I don't know who is talking, but I recognize by his accent that he's a Southerner." Harry said, "That's you, Senator." I responded, "If that's right, I can say for the first time since I went to the Senate, I agree with everything that's being said."

❦ During my years in the Senate I often invoked humor in committee hearings and debate in the Senate.

I introduced proposed constitutional amendments to make the balancing of the federal budget mandatory except in times of war declared by Congress or times of economic depression proclaimed by the votes of two-thirds of the members of each house of Congress. The big spenders were in control, however, and my proposed amendments died aborning.

Congress has not been the sole culprit in federal extravagance. It has been aided and abetted by presidents. After his reelection in 1972, President Nixon began to impound funds appropriated by Congress at his request in appropriation laws signed by him. As chairman of the Senate Government Operations Committee, I took the position that under the Constitution the power of the purse belonged to Congress and that the president had no power to impound funds appropriated by Congress except to the extent Congress had empowered him to do so by the Anti-Deficiency Act or other legislation.

In my judgment the president's power under the Constitution in respect to all congressional acts of which he disapproves is limited to vetoing them and allowing Congress to nullify his veto by a two-thirds majority in each House if it so desires.

Senator Edmund S. Muskie and I introduced a bill to regulate the presidential impoundment of congressionally appropriated funds in conformity with these principles. President Nixon sent Deputy Attorney General Joseph T. Sneed, who had recently been dean at Duke University Law School, to oppose our bill, which was being considered in a joint hearing before the Senate Government Operations Committee and the Senate Subcommittee on Constitutional Rights.

Dean Sneed contended the bill was unconstitutional because the Constitution vested in the president the power to impound congressionally appropriated funds. When I insisted that he specify the constitutional provision that vested this power in the president, the dean claimed that it was given to the president by Article 2, Section 3, which declares that the president "shall take care that the laws be faithfully executed."

I advised the dean that I disagreed with him most emphatically. I said, "The word *execute* is used in different contexts to mean different things. For example, we say when it imposes the death penalty on a capital felon, the State has executed him. But the phrase you invoke as used in Article 2, Section 3, does not empower the president to inflict the death penalty on acts of Congress. It obligates him to carry out acts of Congress—including acts making appropriations—in accordance with the congressional intent.

"Dean, you have striven manfully to confer on the president a nonexistent constitutional power. I pay you a compliment similar to one which a superior court judge paid to me after he had submitted a criminal case defended by me to the jury. He said, 'You have made the best possible argument for an obviously guilty client.'"

In attacking this bill at a meeting with the press, I went on, President Nixon stated that he had to impound funds because Congress was financially irresponsible. At first blush this statement irritated me because I was a member of Congress. My irritation soon vanished, however, because I realized the President had told the truth, but only a half truth. Virtually every president the nation had had since I went to the Senate had also been financially irresponsible in that he had urged Congress to appropriate funds he knew Congress didn't have for causes pleasing to him. And the most financially irresponsible of all of them had been the present occupant of the White House. During President Nixon's first term the national debt increased more than one hundred billion dollars, chiefly as a result of appropriations approved by him.

If President Nixon wanted to persuade Congress to enact his programs, I concluded, he ought to have refrained from charging its members with sole responsibility for fiscal follies shared by him and them. I ended by asking Dean Sneed to convey to the White House my suggestion that there were two things the White House ought to read. One was Dale Carnegie's book *How to Win Friends and Influence People*, and the other was the Constitution of the United States.

During the early 1950s, Senator Joseph R. McCarthy, of Wisconsin, became a terror on the Washington scene by making sensational but unproven charges of Communist subversion in high governmental circles. He acquired a large following in the country at large among those who accept as true unproven charges which frighten them. Besides, he acquired much notoriety by browbeating witnesses who appeared before the Senate Government Operations Committee and the Senate Permanent Subcommittee on Investigations, of which he was chairman.

The Senate, which was the only body possessing the constitutional power to discipline one of its members, ignored McCarthy's boisterous behavior. Senate Republicans were loath to challenge him because his vote constituted the one-vote majority by which they controlled the organization of the Senate. Some senators on both sides of the aisle did not object to his charges because they believed there was some substance to them. As Elmer Davis, a renowned radio commentator of a bygone era, once said, some senators scare easily, and they feared that McCarthy would turn his easily provoked wrath on them and brand them as being soft on Communism if they displeased him. Other senators were simply pragmatic politicians who did not want McCarthy to throw political mud on them.

They emulated the priest and the Levite in the Parable of the Good Samaritan, and passed by in silence on the other side.

A few bold Democratic senators did challenge McCarthy, who, as a shrewd psychologist, comprehended and applied to the hilt the moral of Aesop's fable that whom the gods would destroy they first make mad. McCarthy made mincemeat of them by angering them out of their wits. The arsenals of these senators were unfortunately destitute of humor, the weapon that would have baffled a person of McCarthy's ilk.

Inspired by courageous commentators and journalists, such as Edward R. Murrow, the news media and the public ultimately demanded that the Senate do something to curb McCarthy's actions.

Soon after I became one of its members, the Senate established a select or special committee, composed of three Republican senators —Arthur V. Watkins, of Utah, Frank Carlson, of Kansas, and Francis H. Case, of South Dakota—and three Democratic senators— Edwin C. Johnson, of Colorado, John C. Stennis, of Mississippi, and me—which was directed to investigate proposals to censure Senator McCarthy for disorderly behavior in his senatorial office and to report its findings and recommendations to the Senate in respect to them. The committee was known as the Watkins Committee for its chairman, Senator Watkins, a dour and courageous Mormon.

After dignified—and untelevised—hearings, the Watkins Committee unanimously recommended that the Senate censure McCarthy on two counts for disorderly behavior in his senatorial office. The first count charged that he had contemptuously frustrated the Senate Rules Committee in its efforts to investigate accusations of financial misconduct on his part, and the second count was that he had grossly browbeaten General Ralph W. Zwicker, a witness before the Senate Permanent Subcommittee on Investigations.

The Senate was called into special session to consider the recommendation. After the special session had convened, McCarthy made caustic comments on the session and the Watkins Committee. He called the special session "a lynch party" and the committee "the unwitting handmaiden of the Communist Party." He added that in recommending his censure the committee was acting as "the involuntary agent of Communism."

By way of comment on McCarthy's charges, Ed Johnson, a burly man, said, "I've been accused of many things during my long public career, but this is the first time I've ever been accused of being anybody or anything's handmaiden." I asserted, in substance, that if McCarthy made his charges respecting the committee knowing them to be untrue, he might well be expelled from the Senate for moral incapacity to be a senator, and that if he made them believing them to be true, he might well be expelled from the Senate for mental incapacity to be a senator.

Each member of the Watkins Committee was assigned the task of speaking in favor of its recommendation. I discussed what I should say with my wise aide, Harry Gatton. We agreed that McCarthy was vulnerable to humor, and Harry enjoined me, "Don't forget to tell the Senate about Ephraim Swink."

In speaking to the Senate in favor of the recommendation of the Watkins Committee that the Senate censure McCarthy, I first told the Senate a story to illustrate McCarthy's technique of lifting things out of context to disparage others. "I now know that the lifting of statements out of context is a typical McCarthy technique," I began. "The writer of Ecclesiastes assures us that 'there is nothing new under the sun.' The McCarthy technique of lifting statements out of context was practiced in North Carolina about seventy-five years ago. At that time the women had a habit of wearing their hair in topknots. This preacher deplored that habit. As a consequence, he preached a rip-snorting sermon one Sunday on the text 'Top Not Come Down.' At the conclusion of his sermon an irate woman, wearing a very pronounced topknot, told the preacher that no such text could be found in the Bible. The preacher thereupon opened the Scriptures to the seventeenth verse of the twenty-fourth chapter of Matthew and pointed to the words 'Let him which is on the housetop not come down to take anything out of his house.' Any practitioner of the McCarthy technique of lifting things out of context can readily find the text 'top not come down' in this verse."

My second story was meant to impress upon the Senate its obligation to itself and to our country to adopt the committee's recommendation. "Mr. President, many years ago there was a custom in a section of my county, known as the South Mountains, to hold religious meetings at which the oldest members of the congregation were called upon to stand up and publicly testify to their religious experiences. On one occasion they were holding such a meeting in one of the churches, and old Uncle Ephraim Swink, a South Mountaineer whose body was all bent and distorted with arthritis, was present. All the older members of the congregation except Uncle Ephraim arose and gave testimony to their religious experiences. Uncle Ephraim kept his seat. Thereupon the moderator said, 'Brother Ephraim, suppose you tell us what the Lord has done for you.' Uncle Ephraim arose with his bent and distorted body, and said, 'Brother, he has mighty nigh ruint me.'

"Mr. President, that is about what Senator McCarthy has done to the Senate. As a result of Senator McCarthy's activities and the failure of the Senate to do anything positive about them, the monstrous idea has found lodgement in the minds of millions of loyal and thoughtful Americans that senators are intimidated by Senator McCarthy's threats of libel and slander, and for that reason the will of the Senate to visit upon Senator McCarthy the senatorial discipline he so justly merits is paralyzed.

"The Senate is trying this issue: Was Senator McCarthy guilty of disorderly behavior in his senatorial office? The American people are trying another issue. The issue before the American people transcends in importance the issue before the Senate. The issue before the American people is simply this: Does the Senate of the United States have enough manhood to stand up to Senator McCarthy?

"Mr. President, the honor of the Senate is in our keeping. I pray that senators will not soil it by permitting Senator McCarthy to go unwhipped of senatorial justice."

On December 2, 1954, the Senate substituted for the count relating to Zwicker a second count alleging that McCarthy merited censure for his attacks on the Watkins Committee and the Senate. After so doing, the Senate voted 67 to 22 to censure McCarthy because his conduct as set forth in both counts was "contrary to Senate traditions."

Although the vote for censure did not deprive McCarthy of any of his prerogatives as a senator, it had tremendous impact upon the country at large as well as on McCarthy. After the Senate acted, the press, the politicians, and the people virtually ignored McCarthy and his activities, and his capacity to defame and terrify others effectively ended. As a consequence, his power vanished.

❧   I was a member of the Senate Armed Services Committee. Senator Richard B. Russell, chairman of the committee, appointed a special subcommittee consisting of senators Stuart Symington, Henry M. Jackson, James H. Duff, Leverett Saltonstall, and me to investigate the sufficiency of the air force to perform its mission in national defense.

Charles E. Wilson, the secretary of defense, was an able, sincere, and outspoken individual who had a pronounced capacity to open his mouth and put both of his feet in it. A few days before he appeared before the special subcommittee as a witness, Secretary Wilson had made a characteristic remark at the marine installation in Quantico, Virginia.

Senator Jackson queried Secretary Wilson concerning his unfortunate remark. Secretary Wilson resented Senator Jackson's questions, and Senator Jackson resented the secretary's answers. As a result tension was building up in the subcommittee. To relieve it, I said, "Mr. Secretary, if you and Senator Jackson will forgive me, I'll interrupt you and observe that I oftentimes say things I afterwards regret. For this reason, I appreciate what Jonah is reputed to have said to the whale after he had spent three uncomfortable days in the whale's belly and had been cast up on dry ground. According to an unbiblical tradition, Jonah told the whale, "If you had kept your damned mouth shut, this wouldn't have happened."

The tension was relieved, everybody laughed, and Secretary Wilson asked me, "Have you heard what the mama whale said to her baby?" I said, "No." Secretary Wilson said, "The mama whale told the baby whale it's only when you're blowing that you get harpooned."

❧   For three years I served on the McClellan Rackets Committee, which was named for its chairman, a courageous Arkansas Senator, and which investigated illegal, improper, and unethical activities in the labor-management field. The investigation revealed gross tyrannies practiced by the officers of some unions on their members.

After the McClellan Committee had completed its investigation, I joined Senator John F. Kennedy in introducing the Kennedy-Ervin bill, which was designed in its original version merely to protect unions and rank-and-file union members against corrupt and tyrannical union officers.

While the Kennedy-Ervin bill was being considered by the Senate, Senator Alexander Smith, of New Jersey, a most conscientious legislator, offered a vaguely worded amendment providing that union officers would owe unions and members the obligations of fiduciaries.

As one wedded to the belief that laws ought to specify the obligations they impose in exact terms, I opposed the amendment and suggested that Senator Smith redraft his proposal and state its objective in specific terms. I pointed out that its existing phraseology would produce great confusion because fiduciaries are created and their duties are defined by state laws rather than by acts of Congress.

Senator Gordon Allott, of Colorado, undertook to refute my assertion by quoting references in the index to the United States Code to such fiduciaries as administrators, executors, and trustees.

I recalled a story I had heard one of North Carolina's most gifted trial lawyers, Luther T. Hartsell, tell a Cabarrus County jury years before, and applied it to Senator Allott's argument. His argument, I said, reminded me of a custom which prevailed in rural areas in North Carolina. Once a year people whose departed relatives and friends had been buried in a country churchyard gathered and tidied up their graves by removing briars and weeds from them and planting flowers on them.

A man who shared my aversion to physical labor had hired George, a teenaged youth, to perform this chore in his behalf. Suddenly George guffawed. "George," his employer asked, "what are you laughing about?" "Boss, I'm laughing about the funny words on this gravestone." His employer said, "George, I don't see any funny words on the gravestone." "Look, here, Boss," George responded. "It says 'not dead but sleeping.' He ain't fooling anybody but himself."

"Senator Allott," I explained, "ain't fooling anybody but himself. If he'll read the statutes to which the index to the United States Code refers, he'll discover that they are federal laws that impose obligations such as paying federal income taxes and the like upon state fiduciaries, and he'll stop fooling himself."

❧　By its foreign aid program, the United States has converted itself in large measure into an international Santa Claus who scatters untold billions of dollars of the patrimony of our people among multitudes of foreign nations, some needy and some otherwise, in the pious hope that America can thereby purchase friends and peace in the international world, and induce some foreign nations to reform their internal affairs in ways pleasing to the dispensers of our largess.

I voted for the foreign aid bill during my first year in the Senate on the theory that it was 51 percent wise and 49 percent foolish. Afterward I opposed all foreign aid bills except those which restricted our assistance to needy nations that had indicated their purpose to stand with the free world in any Armageddon with Communism. In opposing foreign aid bills authorizing gifts and loans at low rates of interest, I called the attention of the senators to this wise counsel which Polonius gave to his son Laertes:

> Neither a borrower, nor a lender be;
> For loan oft loses both itself and friend,
> And borrowing dulls the edge of husbandry.

I reminded the senators that every cent our country had expended in financing the foreign aid programs had been obtained by deficit financing. I added, "If an individual were to borrow money to give it away, his family would institute a lunacy proceeding against him and have a guardian named to manage his affairs on the ground he lacked the mental capacity to perform that task himself. But if an American politician advocates that the United States borrow money by deficit financing and scatter it abroad among potential friends and foes alike, he is likely to be elected president or senator or representative, or to be appointed secretary of state or administrator of foreign aid."

After I became silent, the senators invariably ignored my wise counsel and voted overwhelmingly for all foreign aid proposals. With the concurrence of the House over the years, they added billions of dollars to our national debt, and often lost for our country both friends and loans. By so doing, they identified themselves with the answer to John Heywood's question: "Who is so deafe or so blinde as is hee, / That wilfully will neither hear nor see?"

During a period of financial depression, the Senate had under consideration a bill which substantially increased unemployment insurance benefits, which are now euphemistically called employment security benefits. Since the authors of the bill wished to avoid upsetting the political applecart, they provided that the increased benefits would be payable after the bill became law, but that the taxes necessary to finance them would not be levied for some eighteen months—a period beyond the next election.

Senator John Williams, of Delaware, offered an amendment specifying that taxes to finance the increased benefits would become payable at the same time as the increased benefits.

In speaking against the amendment, Senator Joseph S. Clark, of Pennsylvania, looked at me, and said, "The senator from North Carolina knows that our country is now in a depression, and that modern economy teaches that government should make outlays of money to stimulate the economy and refrain from raising taxes in times of depression."

Being thus addressed, I replied, in substance, "There's nothing modern in that theory. There is an apocryphal story to the effect that about one hundred years ago a member of the British Parliament who adhered to that theory introduced a bill in the House of Commons which authorized an enormous bond issue and provided for the immediate expenditure of its proceeds on temporary projects. The bill stipulated further, however, that no payment should be made on the principal of the bonds for fifty years. A member of the House of Commons, whose economic philosophy coincided with mine, condemned the bill on the ground that it was not fair to posterity. The author of the bill replied, 'Posterity hasn't done anything for me, and I don't propose to do anything for it.'"

In recounting this episode afterward, Senator Russell B. Long, of Louisiana, said, "Unfortunately, Senator Ervin fell a little short of statesmanship. He didn't tell the Senate that posterity can't vote in the next election."

Senators and representatives who have been unwilling to do anything for posterity have done a lot to it by giving it runaway inflation and the huge national debt.

ℰ   Rightly interpreted, the Constitution in its present form confers on all Americans of all races equality of constitutional and legal rights and forbids government to frustrate this constitutional objective by making race a criterion for bestowing rights or imposing burdens on any human being within our borders. As a Senator, I opposed civil rights proposals because they frustrated this constitutional objective. They bestow on members of minority races special privileges denied to other Americans. In opposing civil rights bills, I often found myself in forensic combat with Senator Jacob Javits, of New York, an able lawyer and an indefatigable legislator.

I was critical of certain Supreme Court decisions on one occasion, and he intimated that I ought to accept the decisions as valid because I had taken an oath to support the Constitution.

"I have taken an oath to support the Constitution," I replied, "and I shall keep it. But I've never taken an oath to support judicial aberrations, and I shall never accept them as guides for my official action or that of the government. My position in this respect is in complete harmony with that of a great president, who happened to be a Republican. If I remember history aright, Abraham Lincoln had something to say on this subject in the debates in the senatorial contest between him and Stephen A. Douglas. As I recall, Lincoln stated, in essence, 'The Dred Scott decision is erroneous. It is contrary to precedents. I shall do what I can to secure its reversal. Meantime, I refuse to accept it as a guide for my official conduct, and that of the government. I say these things about the Dred Scott decision, notwithstanding I believe it is the duty of the parties to it to obey it.'"

In advocating a certain civil rights proposal, Senator Javits was somewhat critical of the South. At that particular time some students in public schools in New York were committing racially motivated assaults on teachers and fellow students, and police were patrolling school grounds and buildings to suppress the violence.

During the Senate debate I could not resist reminding Senator Javits of those incidents. I then said, "I will not admit that the distinguished senator from New York is qualified to be a physician of racial ills in the South until he cures those on his own doorstep. Until he does that, I will associate him in my mind with a column which Will Rogers wrote for the press."

In his column, I went on to tell the Senate, Will suggested that persons who are ill would be well advised to seek medical treatment by specialists in the field in which their illness lies rather than by general practitioners. After it appeared in the press, he was confined by arthritis to a hospital in Beverly Hills. Shortly afterward, his family doctor from Ardmore, Oklahoma, walked into his hospital room. He said, "Will, you tried to put us old family doctors out of business; I was afraid you'd take your own fool advice, and get a specialist in arthritis to treat you; so I've come all the way to California to look after you until you are on your feet." Will asked his old family doctor, "Do you know anything about arthritis?" He replied, "I sure do. I've been suffering with it myself for fifty years."

Notwithstanding our irreconcilable disagreements in respect to civil rights proposals and our differences on some economic and trade issues, I discovered that Jacob Javits is a truly great American, and I accorded him a soft spot in my heart. He always stood beside me in my fights for the freedom of individuals. After I became bogged down in the Watergate investigation, he went more than the second mile to aid me as chairman of the Senate Government Operations Committee in formulating legislative proposals pending before it for consideration by the Senate.

❧ During 1963, Attorney General Robert F. Kennedy appeared before the Senate Judiciary Committee to present drastic civil rights proposals of the Kennedy administration. As an opponent of these proposals, I was engaged for some days in what the news media called the "Sam and Bobby Show." At the outset, I stated that I could understand why his brother, the President, wished to abolish literacy tests. His signature revealed, I asserted, that he could not write.

The attorney general had a penchant for invoking statistics to sustain his opinions. I undertook to refute the inferences he drew from them by the following anecdote. An old South Mountaineer in Burke County had been buying his groceries on credit from the neighborhood grocer. Believing it time to make payment for them, the old mountaineer asked the grocer for the amount of his bill, and complained with vigor that it was exorbitant when the grocer told him what it was. The grocer thereupon opened his account books, laid them on the counter, and told the old man, "Here are the figures; you know figures don't lie." The old mountaineer responded, "Figures may not lie, but liars sure do figure."

Since I desired my humor to illuminate but not to wound, I hastened to add, "And honest men also figure, and in so doing, often reach incorrect conclusions."

❧ Like many Northerners who advocated civil rights proposals, Attorney General Kennedy had a simple explanation for illiteracy among blacks in the South. Its sole cause, in his view, was state discrimination against blacks in education.

This explanation was too simplistic. The South suffered in times past from much illiteracy among both whites and blacks. Southern states were too poor in the aftermath of the Civil War to maintain adequate schools. The poverty of their parents oftentimes necessitated keeping children out of the inadequate schools that did exist because their labor was essential to the family support. Besides, illiteracy sometimes resulted from laziness or a contempt for education.

Inasmuch as I was the only opponent of his civil rights proposals who habitually appeared at meetings of the Senate Judiciary Committee, the attorney general obviously decided to try to embarrass me by discrediting my home state, North Carolina. He announced that the census of 1960 revealed that North Carolina was the habitat of about thirty thousand illiterate blacks and asserted that such revelation showed that North Carolina discriminated against blacks in education.

I asked him what the census disclosed with respect to the ages of black illiterates in North Carolina. He disclaimed any knowledge of that fact, and I said that North Carolina had had compulsory school attendance laws for many years and that I would surmise that most of the illiterate blacks residing in it were adults when he was born.

After the Senate Judiciary Committee recessed, I studied the census of 1960 for myself. I discovered that my surmise in respect to the ages of black illiterates in North Carolina was correct. I also discovered to my surprise, and to Attorney General Kennedy's consternation, that the census of 1960 disclosed his home state, Massachusetts, numbered among its inhabitants about sixty thousand illiterate whites.

When I made this disclosure to the committee, I assured the attorney general that I did not maintain it proved that Massachusetts discriminated against whites in education.

Chapter 13

More Humor
in the Senate

❦ ❦ ❦

Watson Fairley, a beloved North Carolina Presbyterian preacher, was not overly fond of reformers. He was accustomed to say that if one of them had been standing at the foot of Mount Sinai and had seen the Prophet Moses descending the mountain with the Tablets of Stone which he had just received from the Lord, he would have dashed halfway up the mountain and said, "Wait a minute, Moses, I've got to amend the Ten Commandments before you deliver them to the children of Israel."

The principal targets of those who were bent on reforming the Senate were Rule 22 of the Standing Rules of the Senate and the seniority system. Rule 22 made the Senate the world's most distinctive legislative body by securing to a minority of its members an opportunity to express their views and convert themselves into a majority. Rule 22 bears no rational relationship to the ensuing observation and story.

Progress robs us of past delights. The substitution of travel by automobile for travel by train did that. Before passenger trains virtually vanished from the rails, we could entrust to the engineer the responsibility for watching the road ahead and relax with congenial traveling companions in the luxury of the dining and club cars.

On a faraway evening I boarded the train for an overnight trip to Raleigh. While awaiting the time for retiring to my berth, I joined fellow travelers in the club car. United States Senator Josiah William Bailey monopolized the conversation most of the evening expounding his opinions on public issues. At long last, Senator Bailey confessed, "I haven't been heeding the wise counsel President William Preston Few of Duke University gave me. He said, 'Bailey, a man seldom regrets saying too little.'"

The reformers decried Rule 22 as a rule permitting filibusters. They wanted to convert it into what Senator Dick Russell called a gag rule so they would not be required to listen very long to the expression of views hostile to theirs. I preferred to call Rule 22 a rule authorizing educational debate. If senators who speak at length reflect one's views, they are engaged in educational debate; but if they express views incompatible with one's own, they are filibustering.

I esteemed Rule 22 to be a wise procedural rule. My stand harmonized with that of the late Senator Joseph C. O'Mahoney, of Wyoming, who was a true liberal, and who opposed all proposals to make it easier for the majority to silence the minority. He asserted that protracted Senate debate had often defeated bad legislative schemes, and had often made originally unwise bills otherwise by producing ameliorating amendments. He maintained, however, that no good legislation had ever been defeated for long by protracted debate.

As it existed during my Senate days, Rule 22 provided, in essence, that debate "upon any measure, motion, or other matter pending before the Senate" could not "be brought to a close" unless "two-thirds of the Senators present and voting" adopted a cloture motion signed by sixteen senators.

Senator Frank Church, of Idaho, who led the reformers in one session in their efforts to make it possible for an impatient majority to silence a minority by less than "two-thirds of the Senators present and voting" obtained an erroneous interpretation of Rule 22 from Vice-President Hubert H. Humphrey, who was presiding.

Senator Church asked the Vice-President for a ruling on the question as to what the consequences would be if a majority of the senators present and voting voted in favor of a cloture motion, but such majority was less than two-thirds of those present and voting. The Vice-President made a ruling incompatible with the words of Rule 22. He adjudged that in such event debate in the Senate would end.

Senator Spessard L. Holland, of Florida, appealed Vice-President Humphrey's ruling to the Senate. Such stalwart senators as George Aiken and Margaret Chase Smith supported his appeal, and the Senate rejected the ruling by a substantial vote.

In supporting the appeal, I could not forbear saying, "A young fellow, whom I shall call Frank, met an old friend, whom I shall call Hubert. Hubert was wearing a beautiful sweater with the huge letter K emblazoned on it. Frank asked Hubert, 'What does the letter K mean?' Hubert replied, 'Confused.' Frank said, 'You don't spell confused with a K.' Hubert responded, 'If you are as confused as I am, you do.'"

The Adlai Ewing Stevenson family of Illinois had its early American roots in Iredell County, North Carolina, where some of their distant relatives still reside. My colleague, Senator Adlai E. Stevenson III, who advocated softening what he deemed to be the rigor of Rule 22, assumed the task of presiding in the Senate when I was speaking in opposition to the pending proposal to change Rule 22. I had among my verbal ammunition a marvelous statement made by his great-grandfather, the original Adlai E. Stevenson, while he was serving as vice-president under Grover Cleveland. The statement extolled with Stevenson eloquence the Senate of his day for its wisdom in allowing unlimited debate.

I read the statement to the Senate and asserted that the presiding officer's great-grandfather was a great statesman who undoubtedly owed much of his wisdom to his family's roots in North Carolina.

Senator Stevenson came to my desk the next day and made a statement which revealed much of the Stevenson wit. He said, "You demonstrated in your speech of yesterday that the Stevensons have deteriorated intellectually in proportion to the space and time they have put between themselves and North Carolina."

Rule 22 has blessed the Senate and the country. It has protected the minority against the tyranny of the majority in the Senate. It has afforded wise minorities opportunities to convert erring majorities to their sound views. It has safeguarded the country at times against hasty and intemperate demands of politically powerful selfish groups and special interests.

The rule has been weakened since I left the Senate. Those who seek to weaken it further would do well to pause and ponder certain truths. As history demonstrates, the first act of a dictator who wants to cement his domination of his land is to suppress dissenting legislators. Any rule which can be invoked today to gag a troublesome demagogue can be used tomorrow to silence a patriot speaking in behalf of a just cause.

꙳ My brilliant colleague Senator Joseph S. Clark, of Pennsylvania, and I were good friends, notwithstanding our differing views of the Senate as a legislative institution. Joe was convinced that the rules and traditions of the Senate were as outmoded as the age that produced the Neanderthal Man.

Joe introduced an ingenious resolution which was aimed directly at the heart of the Senate seniority system. The resolution specified, in essence, that no senator was eligible to hold the chairmanship of a Senate committee unless his views in respect to matters of which the committee had initial jurisdiction coincided with the position taken by his party's platform on such matters.

As I heard Joe explain his resolution to the Senate and urge its adoption, my resolve not to say a murmuring word about it vanished, and I was constrained to voice my opposition to it.

In the first place, I said, many platform provisions are written to conceal rather than reveal a party's position on controversial issues. They duplicate what Herbert Hoover said about the repeal of the Eighteenth Amendment in 1928. My candidate, Governor Alfred E. Smith, was an outspoken advocate of repeal. Hoover was silent on the subject until the people demanded that he make his position clear. The Republican National Committee thereupon announced with fanfare that Hoover would make his position plain in a speech at Elizabethton, Tennessee. All he said on the subject in that speech was that "prohibition is a noble experiment." This statement served its baffling purpose well. Those who favored repeal said, "Hoover is for repeal. An experiment is something which fails." Those who opposed repeal were equally pleased. They declared, "Hoover opposes repeal. He said prohibition is noble."

In the second place, I continued, most party platforms are not as secretive as Hoover was at Elizabethton. They promise everybody everything they want, no matter how contradictory those promises may be. Although I was not allowed to write many of its words, I sat on the subcommittee that drafted the Democratic party's platform at a recent national convention. The platform pledged, in effect, that the party was going to give everybody everything they wanted out of the empty federal treasury, and simultaneously to balance the federal budget.

If the resolution of the Senator from Pennsylvania were incorporated in the Senate rules, the following events would likely ensue: Senator A offers a bill to appropriate billions of dollars for a cause he espouses. Senator B, the chairman of the committee to which the bill is referred, opposes the bill. Senator A demands that Senator B be removed from his chairmanship because his views respecting the bill do not coincide with the platform's pledge to give everybody everything they want out of the empty treasury, and Senator B insists that his views do coincide with the platform's pledge to balance the budget and that A's bill, if enacted, would make it impossible to balance the budget.

Since the resolution contains nothing that would solve either of these dilemmas, I concluded, it creates more problems than it solves. The resolution was rejected.

❧   Opponents of congressional seniority invariably portray chairmen of committees as doddering old idiots. Although on rare occasions the chairman of a congressional committee may hold on to his position a little too long, the charge that opponents of seniority make in this respect is ordinarily without any foundation. Indeed, virtually all congressional committee chairmen are highly intelligent and have accumulated over the years unsurpassed knowledge in respect to the matters of which their committees have initial jurisdiction. As Woodrow Wilson once said, "Congress in committee is Congress at work."

The seniority system is an illustration of the truth that experience is the most efficient teacher of all things. In defending the system, Senator Alben W. Barkley said, "The seniority system may be subject to some just criticism. What Winston Churchill is reputed to have said about Democracy may apply to it. Churchill is reputed to have said that 'Democracy is the world's worst form of government, except every other government which has ever been tried.' I'll stick to the seniority system until somebody is smart enough to devise a better one."

❦ Senator Barkley was one of America's most captivating story-tellers. The Senate was debating a bill to raise the salaries of senators and representatives. Barkley was sitting in the Democratic cloakroom. Another senator asked him how he was going to vote. Barkley replied, "I'm going to vote for the bill. I'm not going to be a damned fool the second time in the same respect."

Barkley then related how he had defeated a similar proposal in the House some years before, and how he had returned to his home in Paducah with the fervent expectation that his constituents would welcome him with a brass band to voice their approval of his valiant defeat of the iniquitous attempt of senators and representatives to raid the Treasury.

When he got home, he narrated, no brass band met him; in fact, no constituent ever mentioned to him his glorious defeat of the attempted raid.

Sometime later, he related, he began his customary tour of his district. When he visited a mercantile establishment in a rural community, its owner, a loyal personal and political friend, asked him, "What did you do in the last Congress?"

Barkley said, "I told my friend with much pride how I had fought, bled, and died defeating the proposed raid on the Treasury."

His friend, he related, looked at him right hard, and asked, "Alben, are you telling me you had a chance to vote to raise your own salary, and you voted against it?"

Barkley said he told his friend, "That's exactly what I'm telling you"; and his friend declared, "Well, Alben, you're a damned fool."

Barkley added, "I'm not going to be a damned fool again."

❦ The surgeon general convinced himself that he possessed all the truth respecting the smoking of cigarettes and that those who denied his pontifical pronouncements on the subject possessed none. It became my lot to defend the economic interests of North Carolina tobacco growers and manufacturers in the Senate against the attacks of those whom the surgeon general had persuaded that all lung cancer is the result of the smoking of cigarettes, even when it victimizes those who have never smoked.

In conformity with my usual practice, I made a laborious and painstaking study of the subject. Although it did not satisfy me that cigarette smoking is as healthy as the consumption of yogurt, my study did convince me that many competent physicians disagree with the surgeon general's views. Moreover, I found that known medical facts relating to the time of the incidence of lung cancer and differences in the sexes of its victims conflicted with them, that the statistics he invoked to support them were snatched out of the empty air, and that there was no substantial clinical evidence to sustain them.

In reporting these findings in a speech to the Senate, I referred to a bit of doggerel verse I had found in a medical journal. This verse epitomized the current propensity of governmental officials and some self-confessed experts on health to ascribe cancer and virtually all other ills of the flesh to the things we eat, drink, and smoke. It closed with the assertion that if we would only avoid their use, we would not have to worry about anything except a sudden bolt of lightning from the sky, and we could die of malnutrition with our arteries intact.

On a subsequent occasion senators from tobacco-growing states were opposing the proposal to place a warning on packs of cigarettes. I observed during the discussion that no one had suggested that the government should put any warnings on containers of intoxicating liquors.

Senator Thurston Morton, of Kentucky, hurried to my Senate desk and observed, "It's bad enough for Kentucky's enemies to attack one of its chief economic products—tobacco. It's even worse for one of Kentucky's friends to attack her other chief economic product—bourbon liquor." I assured Thurston I would not commit my offense a second time.

❦ The most precious emolument of a senator is the genial companionship he enjoys with other members of what is called the nation's most exclusive club. A senator is able to enjoy such companionship with a colleague with whom he disagrees most drastically on public issues when he understands his background and motivation.

I enjoyed particularly sharing hours of labor and moments of leisure with Senator John C. Stennis, of Mississippi, whom I esteem to be one of America's greatest public servants and one of the Senate's most gifted raconteurs. He tells a story of a candidate for the Mississippi Legislature who promised to give the earth and the fullness thereof to his constituents if they would make him their choice. When he confronted him in debate, his adversary asserted it would take much money to fulfill his promise and put to him these politically embarrassing inquiries: "Where are you going to get all that money? Are you going to raise the taxes of your constituents?" "No, no, by golly," he replied. "I'm not going to raise anybody's taxes. I'm going to do like Congress does when it wants to spend money it hasn't got. I'll appropriate it, by golly, I'll appropriate it."

❧ Another of his stories is about the justice of the peace who tried petty cases in DeKalb County, Mississippi. The justice decided a petty civil case adversely to an attorney, who had the reputation of being irascible. The attorney managed to control his temper for the moment and requested the justice to let him know when his court had adjourned.

After recording his judgment on the docket, the justice informed the attorney that court had adjourned. The lawyer thereupon denounced the justice and his ruling in vitriolic phrases. The justice fined the attorney ten dollars for contempt of his court. The attorney protested the fine, saying the justice had no jurisdiction to impose it because his court had adjourned. The justice said, "Sir, you must understand that irrespective of whether my court is sitting or is in adjournment, it is always an object of contempt."

❧ The story of the DeKalb justice of the peace calls to mind the tale of the deaf lawyer who argued a motion before an impatient judge. The judge ordered the lawyer to sit down. The deaf lawyer, who did not hear the order, proceeded with his argument, and the impatient judge announced in a louder tone of voice that he fined him ten dollars for contempt of court in disobeying the order.

The deaf lawyer realized that the judge had spoken, but he did not comprehend what he had said. He thereupon asked the judge what he had said, and the judge told him to ask the clerk of the court. The deaf lawyer put his question to the clerk, and the clerk informed him that the judge had fined him ten dollars for contempt of court. The deaf lawyer handed a twenty-dollar bill to the clerk and said, "Keep the change. I've got twice as much contempt for the court as the judge thinks I have."

꜊   According to Senator Stennis, a vacancy occurred in a federal district judgeship in the congressional district of Mississippi represented in the House by my friend the late William M. Colmer, of Pascagoula. After Senators Stennis and James O. Eastland had tentatively decided to recommend one of Bill's constituents to the President to fill the vacancy, Senator Stennis visited Bill to ascertain whether their tentative selection met with his approval.

Bill assured Senator Stennis that he was delighted with the proposed selection. In an ensuing colloquy, he said, "John, I've never wanted to be a federal district judge, because federal district judges have to know the law, and I don't know any law. I am compelled to confess, however, that I've always aspired to be a justice of the Supreme Court of the United States. I'm well qualified for that office."

꜊   Two of my most jovial colleagues in the Senate were Robert Samuel Kerr, of Oklahoma, and Theodore Francis Green, of Rhode Island. Both of them were rather partisan Democrats.

Richard M. Nixon, who was then serving as vice-president, was presiding in the Senate when the vote came on a bill involving a hot political issue; it was rejected by one vote—Senator Green's. Knowing that Nixon was bent on concealing from all men his position on the issue, Senator Green changed his vote and forced Nixon to vote to break the resulting tie.

The senator had the reputation of attending all cocktail parties in Washington. An acquaintance saw him at a cocktail party one evening and asked, "Senator Green, how many cocktail parties have you been to this evening?" Senator Green replied, "This is my fourth," and pulled a little notebook from his pocket and began leafing through it. The acquaintance inquired, "Are you trying to ascertain where you are going next?" "No," Senator Green responded, "I'm trying to learn where I am now."

An importunate waiter at a banquet insisted on serving coffee to

Senator Green, who repeatedly advised him he did not want any coffee. Finally, he told the waiter most emphatically he would not drink any coffee by saying, "If I drink coffee, I'll stay awake and have to listen to the speeches."

Once when Senator Green and I were lunching in the private lunchroom of the Senate, Bob Kerr joined us and told Green, "Theodore, I've just visited Rhode Island. Your constituents told me you've espoused awful radical views and become a regular Red." "They're wrong, Bob," Senator Green replied instantly. "I'm not a Rhode Island Red. I'm a Rhode Island Green."

Bob Kerr loved to launch sarcastic darts at Republicans. This was one of his favorite stories.

An incorrigible Oklahoma Republican of prominence had attained the age of ninety-six years. On the anniversary of his birth, he was interviewed by a reporter, who observed, "You've lived a long time, and have seen many changes." The ancient Republican responded, "Yes, and I was against every damned one of them."

I have heard, but never verified, this tale. Bob Kerr was opposed in one of his campaigns for the Senate by a Republican who was a minister of the gospel. They engaged in a joint debate in which the Republican candidate spoke first.

He said, "I believed in times past that seeking public office was incompatible with my holy profession. I became a candidate for the Senate only after I spent the night wrestling in prayer with the Lord and being told by Him that it was my duty to run for the office."

In reply, Kerr said, "A senator holds a most important office. If he is rightly motivated, he can do much good for God and country. Hence, I can conceive of the possibility that the Almighty might urge an individual to run for the Senate. It's inconceivable, however, that the Almighty would tell anyone to run for the Senate on the Republican ticket."

Soon after the Supreme Court handed down its school prayer cases, President Johnson named Nicholas D. Katzenbach attorney general and Ramsey Clark deputy attorney general. After their confirmation, the Federal Bar Association of the District of Columbia gave a luncheon in their honor and requested me to serve as master of ceremonies.

On arriving at the luncheon, I ascertained that Chief Justice Warren was to be my right-hand luncheon companion and observed five or six of the other justices among the luncheon guests. I said to myself in the words of the old hymn, "This is the day I long have sought, and wept because I found it not."

When it became appropriate for me as master of ceremonies to make some remarks, I said the following, as best I can reconstruct from memory:

"I'm always delighted to be with lawyers for several reasons. One is they always furnish such congenial companionship. Another reason, which I may not be permitted to state in the presence of the chief justice and his associates, is that when lawyers pray—which is seldom—they pray with such sincerity. This observation is illustrated by the story of the young lawyer who attended an evangelic service and was unexpectedly called on to pray. He prayed this prayer which came straight from his lawyer heart: 'Stir up much strife among thy people, Lord, lest thy servant perish.'

"An old hymn says, 'The Lord moves in mysterious ways his wonders to perform.' It may be surprising to the chief justice and his associates to be told that the Lord uses even them as an instrument to answer the young lawyer's prayer. When they hand down a decision, as they usually do, in which five of them reach the same legal conclusion after traveling five separate and irreconcilable legal paths and their four brethren dissent from the conclusion on four mutually repugnant grounds, they stir up much strife among the Lord's people and provoke much litigation, and thus answer the young lawyer's prayer effectively. But when the Supreme Court undertakes to explain in a new case what it meant in a former case, it makes confusion more confounded than ever and answers the young lawyer's prayer much more effectively.

"It is indeed fortunate for the American bar that the Supreme Court cannot explain its former decisions with the clarity with which a North Carolina schoolteacher recently explained their school prayer cases. On entering her classroom a few minutes early one morning, she saw a bunch of schoolboys down on their knees in a huddle in a corner of the room. She asked in a stern voice, 'What are you boys doing?' One of them answered, 'We're shooting craps.' She responded, 'That's all right. I was afraid you were praying.'"

🦫 During our twenty years in Washington my wife and I frequently relaxed in the evenings by dining with friends and attending banquets and receptions given by various groups. One of the most delightful of the banquets was that of the Jefferson Island Club honoring three great Americans, former president Harry S. Truman, former vice-president Alben W. Barkley, and Speaker of the House Sam Rayburn.

Each of the honored guests made humorous remarks. Those of Barkley were particularly entrancing. He said, in substance, "President Truman and I are alike in one respect. Whenever someone makes us mad, we write him letters. Our similarity stops there. President Truman runs to the nearest mailbox and mails his letter. I put my letter in my desk, keep it there a week, tear it up, and throw its scraps into the wastepaper basket. I wrote a letter to Westbrook Pegler, however, some years ago, which I certainly wish I had mailed to him."

Westbrook Pegler was a widely read syndicated commentator of a few years ago who was noted for his vitriolic attacks on Democrats in general and members of the Franklin D. Roosevelt family in particular.

"When I was vice-president," Barkley continued, "an enthusiastic friend in the House introduced a resolution authorizing the striking of a medal in my honor and requesting the president to present the medal to me. Nobody expected the resolution to emerge from the House committee to which it was referred. One day, however, the House committee reported the resolution favorably, the House approved it, and the Senate suspended its rules and passed it.

"After the medal had been struck, President Truman summoned me to the White House and conferred the medal on me with a few well-chosen words. I undertook to accept it with a few chosen words. It turned out, however, that my words were not well chosen. I said I did not know why I was being given the medal. Westbrook Pegler wrote a column in which he stated that I was not alone in my ignorance. Nobody else had any idea why I was being given the medal, and he suggested I have the medal melted down and apply the gold in it on the national debt. His column angered me, and I wrote him a letter which I wish, in retrospect, I had mailed to him instead of tearing it up and putting the scraps in the waste basket. I told Westbrook Pegler that I was going to have the medal melted down, but was not going to apply the gold in it on the national debt. Instead of doing that, I said, I'm going to give the gold to you because if you get paid in proportion to the truth you tell, you must be in destitute circumstances."

᷏ᷓ   After I left the Senate, my wife and I were invited to Sweden, where I was guest speaker on several occasions during Upsala University's celebration of the five hundredth anniversary of its founding.

Before going to Upsala, I had feared that I might need someone to interpret what I said to the Swedes. On my arrival in Sweden, I ascertained that English is taught to Swedes in school and that they speak and understand English without difficulty.

Subsequently, I met at Hollywood, California, a television tycoon from England who asked me if I could understand Swedes speaking English. "Yes, indeed," I said, "I can understand Swedes speaking English much better than I can Englishmen."

᷏ᷓ   Federal departments and agencies sometimes carry to absurdity the practice of stamping documents "top secret," "secret," and "confidential." Oftentimes they are motivated by a desire to conceal stupidity rather than to protect national security. The crowning achievement in this area was that of the commander of a military unit who had copies of the Constitution stamped with this disclaimer: "This document does not necessarily reflect the views of the commander of this unit."

Chapter 14

Humor in the Watergate Investigation

ଈ ଈ ଈ

On February 7, 1973, Democratic and Republican senators unanimously adopted a resolution drafted by me at the request of Senator Mike Mansfield, the majority leader of the Senate, creating the Select Committee on Presidential Campaign Activities to investigate the burglary of the offices of the Democratic National Committee in the Watergate on June 17, 1972, and other illegal or unethical events occurring during the presidential election of 1972.

The committee consisted of four Democrats, Senators Herman E. Talmadge, Daniel K. Inouye, Joseph M. Montoya, and me, and three Republican senators, Howard H. Baker, Jr., Edward J. Gurney, and Lowell P. Weicker, Jr., who were appointed by the Vice-President on the recommendations of Senator Mansfield and Senator Hugh Scott, the minority leader of the Senate. I served as its chairman, and Howard Baker as its vice-chairman.

Samuel Dash, the committee's chief counsel, Rufus L. Edmisten, its deputy chief counsel, and Arthur S. Miller, principal consultant, were elected by the committee on my recommendation. Fred D. Thompson, the minority counsel, was named by the Republican members of the committee. They and the other members of the committee staff greatly aided the committee in its investigatory labors.

Senator Mansfield gave these reasons for selecting me to be chairman: I had had more judicial experience than any other senator; I was "the most nonpartisan Democrat in the Senate"; and nobody could justly accuse me of harboring presidential or vice-presidential aspirations.

The committee was required to investigate allegations of illegal or unethical conduct on the part of some of the governmental and political aides engaged in furthering President Nixon's reelection, and even allegations that subsequent to the Watergate burglary President Nixon aided and abetted such aides in hiding the truth about their misconduct and the burglary from law enforcement officers, the press, and the people.

As a result, the investigation was probably more surcharged with political emotions and overtones than any other investigation in the nation's history. Despite this circumstance, the Democratic and Republican senators constituting the committee conducted a fair and full investigation of all the facts available to them concerning the matters they were authorized to investigate, joined in a final report respecting their findings, and united in recommendations concerning legislation they deemed appropriate.

Since the investigation has been detailed by many authors and this is a book on humor, I confine further references to the Watergate to humorous incidents, the contempt for constitutional, legal, and ethical principles exhibited by the Nixon White House in its relations to Daniel J. Ellsberg, and the story of President Nixon's secret tapes. The last two subjects reveal the nature and consequences of the Watergate tragedy.

❦ My wife and I resided in an apartment in the Methodist Building in Washington. Our telephone was listed in the Washington telephone directory because we believed that public servants ought to be available to their constituents at all times. Occasionally, we were rudely awakened in the wee hours of the morning by calls from concerned individuals who had perhaps had a bit too much to drink and felt a need to unburden themselves concerning what they called affairs of state. We endured these tribulations with fortitude as the price of maintaining my accessibility to my constituents.

When I was named chairman of the Senate committee to investigate Watergate, however, we began to be plagued with calls at all hours of the night from all areas of the nation, including distant Alaska and Hawaii. Many of these were from representatives of the news media. Others came from persons who simply desired to speak with someone who had suddenly had notoriety thrust upon him. A few came from individuals who can most accurately be described as unusual.

One of the last group, a self-described minister of the Gospel, called me virtually every night from some place in Kentucky and talked thirty or forty minutes. He was in daily communication with the Almighty, he said, and the Almighty had appointed him to pass on to me each day what the Almighty had told him that day about Watergate.

One fact that my informant said the Almighty had told him about Watergate made a poor case for the theological doctrine of the omniscience of God: He said the Almighty told him the chief culprit in Watergate was one of the innocents, Vice-President Spiro T. Agnew.

During one of our calls I asked my informant if he would make a supplication to the Almighty in my behalf. He assured me he would be pleased to do so. I then made this request of him: "Please ask the Good Lord to make his revelations about Watergate directly to me. Inasmuch as the Good Lord has to look after this earth, all its inhabitants, and the entire universe, he couldn't possibly spend as much time talking about the Watergate as you do." My request seemed to offend him, but he must not have taken it to heart, for the next night he was calling me again.

This time he said he wanted the Senate committee to call him as the first witness in the hearings, which were scheduled to begin in a few days. He had just talked to the Almighty about this, he said, and the Almighty had instructed him to tell me to call him first. I answered that I hated to disobey the Almighty's instruction; the committee would be delighted to welcome the Almighty as the lead-off witness, but it couldn't permit him to enact that role in the Almighty's stead because he didn't know anything about Watergate except what the Almighty had told him, and the persons being investigated by the committee would object to his testimony because it was hearsay.

No sooner had he hung up and I sat down than our phone rang again. My wife answered it this time, and it was the Kentucky preacher calling again. Taking advantage of his opportunity to press his suit before a new listener, the preacher told her he believed it would be all right with the Almighty for him to relay to her what He had said that day about Watergate and let her recount it to me.

My wife, who is one of God's most patient creations, listened to him until he hung up. She then said, "We'll get an unlisted telephone tomorrow." We did, and our repose in the future was more peaceful than it had been in the recent past.

❧ The Pentagon Papers were a classified secret synopsis of American involvement in South Vietnam. They had been prepared by the Rand Corporation and others at the instance of the Department of Defense. As an employee of Rand, Daniel J. Ellsberg had had access to the Pentagon Papers. In violation of their classified status, he released copies of them to the *New York Times* and the *Washington Post*, which began to publish them serially in June, 1971.

The Nixon White House insinuated that Ellsberg had also made copies of the Pentagon Papers available to Russia, although no proof to that effect was ever produced and Ellsberg vigorously denied doing so. Ellsberg also stoutly maintained that the release of the Pentagon Papers did not impair in any way the national security of the United States. Secretary of Defense Melvin Laird apparently corroborated this view in large measure because he is reputed to have informed President Nixon that 98 percent of the contents of the Pentagon Papers could have been declassified and made public without threat to the security of the nation.

President Nixon and Henry A. Kissinger, head of the National Security Council and the president's chief foreign affairs adviser, were infuriated by Ellsberg's release of the papers to the *Times* and *Post*. Their infuriation was shortly thereafter intensified by the actions of others who secretly leaked to the press classified governmental information of a highly sensitive nature.

Nixon believed that these events were committed by political enemies seeking to destroy him politically, and he and Kissinger shared the fear that they might engender in the Chinese and Russian minds the conviction that the American government was incapable of keeping secrets and cause them to end secret negotiations then in progress designed to produce the Salt I treaty and the resumption of diplomatic relations between the United States and mainland China.

Acting at the command of President Nixon, the Department of Justice sought injunctions from the United States District Court for the District of Columbia to forbid the further publication by the *New York Times* and the *Washington Post* of the Pentagon Papers; John D. Ehrlichman, the president's chief domestic policy adviser, established a special investigations unit in the White House itself; the FBI wiretapped the telephone of Ellsberg and the telephones of various federal employees and newsmen; and the Department of Justice induced the grand jury sitting in a district court in California to indict Ellsberg on two criminal counts for possession and release of the Pentagon Papers.

In a 6–3 decision, the Supreme Court repudiated the Department of Justice's effort to enjoin the further publication of the Pentagon Papers on the ground that it had failed to prove that their publication would endanger national security.

Ehrlichman established the special investigations unit in the White House at Nixon's directions without authority of law because the White House was convinced that the lawful investigating body, the FBI, would not produce information the White House desired concerning Ellsberg and others.

As the designated head of the special investigations unit, Ehrlichman placed two young White House aides, David Young and Egil Krogh, in active charge of the unit's operations. Charles ("Chuck") Colson, who was often called the White House "hatchet man," offered them much advice and assistance. At his and Ehrlichman's suggestion, they hired E. Howard Hunt, Colson's White House consultant, and G. Gordon Liddy to aid them.

The special investigations unit was a secret group with offices in the Executive Office Building. Its assigned mission was to "stop security leaks and to investigate other sensitive security matters."

After its creation, President Nixon told Colson, "I don't give a damn how it is done, do whatever has to be done to stop these leaks and prevent further unauthorized disclosures; I don't want to be told why it can't be done. This government cannot survive, it cannot function, if anyone can run out and leak whatever documents he wants to. I want to know who is behind this and I want the most complete investigation that can be conducted. I don't want excuses. I want results. I want it done, whatever the cost."

Since the unit was created to stop leaks, its members became known as the Plumbers.

Notwithstanding Ellsberg was being prosecuted in court, the Nixon White House was bent on amassing all derogatory information concerning him and using it to discredit him publicly. Ellsberg had received psychiatric treatment from Dr. Lewis Fielding of Beverly Hills, California, in times past, and the White House was exceedingly desirous of obtaining Dr. Fielding's medical files relating to Ellsberg's mental or emotional state. An effort to obtain such files through the FBI failed because Dr. Fielding had obeyed his Hippocratic oath and refused to reveal them.

The Plumbers recommended to Ehrlichman on August 11, 1971, "that a covert operation be undertaken to examine all the medical files still held by Ellsberg's psychoanalyst covering the 2-year period in which he was under analysis." Ehrlichman approved the recommendation in writing and added these words: "If done under your assurance that it is not traceable."

Ehrlichman denied, however, that he thereby authorized the Plumbers to burglarize Dr. Fielding's office. He insisted that he merely intended that the investigators seeking Dr. Fielding's medical files relating to Ellsberg would not reveal their identities as investigators of the White House or anything of that kind and that they would obtain the highly confidential psychiatric records relating to Ellsberg from nurses or nurses' aides.

Young and Krogh construed Ehrlichman's approval otherwise and commissioned Hunt and Liddy to burglarize Dr. Fielding's office in quest of the files relating to Ellsberg. Acting through three hired accomplices of Cuban ancestry, Bernard L. Barker, Eugenio R. Martinez, and Felipe De Diego, they procured the consummation of the burglary on the night of September 3, 1971. The three hired burglars surreptitiously broke into and ransacked Dr. Fielding's offices. They did not find the medical files relating to Ellsberg, however, because Dr. Fielding had wisely stored them elsewhere. The Nixon White House concealed the burglary from the Department of Justice, Ellsberg's attorneys, and the district court in California where the indictments against Ellsberg were pending.

When he appeared before the Senate Select Committee in July,

1973, Ehrlichman was an exceedingly angry and recalcitrant witness, who bitterly resented the cross-examination to which he was subjected by Chief Counsel Sam Dash, and Senators Talmadge, Inouye, Weicker, and me. He asserted that Young and Krogh had misinterpreted his approval and disclaimed any responsibility in the subsequent action of the Plumbers or their accomplices who had burglarized Dr. Fielding's offices.

Although he asserted that Nixon denied authorizing the burglary, Ehrlichman strongly insisted that the president has the inherent power under the Constitution to authorize burglaries, such as the Fielding break-in, whenever, in his unreviewable discretion, he decides that such action protects the national security. Moreover, he quoted President Nixon as having declared in March, 1973, that this particular break-in "was an important, vital national security, well within the constitutional function of the president."

Ehrlichman's position was absurd. The Plumbers were White House vigilantes possessing no legal authority whatever. They committed a forcible, surreptitious, and warrantless entry of a psychiatrist's office to seize legally confidential psychiatric records relating to his patient. Under the law, those records could not have been admitted in evidence in any court in America without the consent of the patient unless the presiding judge ruled their admission was essential to the doing of justice in a pending case. The Plumbers were not seeking the records for use as evidence in court or to protect national security. They were seeking them solely because they hoped to use them "to destroy the image and credibility" of the patient, who was awaiting trial on criminal charges.

Ehrlichman and his attorneys invoked the act of Congress embodied in 18 U.S.C. 2511 to support his contention that the president has inherent power under the Constitution to authorize burglaries to protect the national security.

I pointed out that, subject to enumerated exceptions, this statute merely makes interceptions of specified wire and oral communications crimes. The exceptions relating to the president confer no statutory powers, and the statute has no possible application to surreptitious entries unrelated to interceptions of the specified communications.

Ehrlichman and his attorneys responded that Congress had acknowledged the inherent constitutional power of the president to authorize surreptitious entries, such as the Fielding break-in, in its enactment of one of the statutory exceptions in 18 U.S.C. 2511. According to that act, "nothing in this chapter or in section 605 of the Communications Act of 1934 . . . shall limit the constitutional power of the President to take such measures as he deems necessary . . . to protect national security information against foreign intelligence activities."

I responded, "Foreign intelligence activities had nothing to do with the opinion of Ellsberg's psychiatrist about his intellectual or emotional or psychological state."

Ehrlichman asked, "How do you know that, Mr. Chairman?"

I replied, "Because I understand the English language. It is my mother tongue."

Attorney John J. Wilson, Ehrlichman's leading counsel, and I thereupon had this exchange:

Wilson: The CIA must have thought that it had some foreign relationship because they have done an ineffective profile on Ellsberg.

Ervin: Well, the CIA had no business doing that because the law prohibits them from having anything to do with internal security.

Wilson: Sir, you would not consider that foreign intelligence activity is—

Ervin: No, it was a domestic intelligence activity. These people were from the Plumbers, from the White House, doing this.

Wilson: We had a man passing secrets to the Soviet government.

Ervin: Well, Ellsberg's psychiatrist wasn't doing that.

In making and possessing his records of Ellsberg's psychiatric state, I asserted, Dr. Fielding was not engaged in "foreign intelligence activities"; and in seeking to obtain those records by a forcible, surreptitious, and warrantless entry, the Plumbers were not protecting "national security information against foreign intelligence activities," even if they acted with the approval of President Nixon. They were committing a rank burglary in violation of the Fourth Amendment.

Under the Constitution, I asserted, the president had no power arbitrarily to suspend any of its provisions. He had only those powers expressly stated and those necessarily implied from those stated. The Constitution was written that way, I declared, to restrain the president from tyranny.

Attorney Wilson had successfully represented one of the steel companies in the famous steel seizure case. In that case the Supreme Court held that nothing in the Constitution granted President Truman the power to seize the steel mills during the Korean War. Calling attention to that case, I observed: "I think that is authority that if the president has no inherent power to seize steel mills to carry on a war, he has no inherent power to steal a document from a psychiatrist's office in time of peace."

࿓ When Ehrlichman and his attorneys and the Senate committee resumed the debate of this subject on the following day, Senator Talmadge was especially sharp in his questioning of Ehrlichman. Did the alleged inherent power that allowed the president to authorize covert break-ins, he asked, extend to murder, robbery, and other crimes? Ehrlichman had to admit that it was difficult to draw the line.

Talmadge and Ehrlichman thereupon had this exchange:

> Talmadge: Do you remember when we were in law school we studied a famous principle of law that came from England, and also is well known in this country, that no matter how humble a man's cottage is, that even the king of England cannot enter without his consent.
>
> Ehrlichman: I am afraid that has been considerably eroded over the years, has it not?
>
> Talmadge: Down in my country we still think it is a pretty legitimate principle of law.

This prompted me to observe:

But I do want to take this occasion to amplify the legal discussion and I want to mention a little of the Bible, a little of history, and a little of law.

The concept embodied in the phrase "Every man's home is his castle" represents the realization of one of the most ancient and universal hungers of the human heart. One of the prophets described the mountain of the Lord as being a place where every man might dwell under his own vine and fig tree with none to make him afraid.

And then this morning, Senator Talmadge talked about one of the greatest statements ever made by any statesman, William Pitt the Elder. Before this country revolted against the king of England he said this: "The poorest man in his cottage may bid defiance to all the forces of the crown. It may be frail, its roof may shake, the wind may blow through it, the storm may enter, the rain may enter, but the King of England cannot enter. All his force dares not cross the threshold of the ruined tenement."

And yet we are told here today, and yesterday, that what the king of England can't do, the president of the United States can.

The greatest decision that the Supreme Court of the United States has ever handed down in my opinion is that of *Ex Parte Milligan* which is reported in 4 Wallace 2, and the things I want to mention appear on page 121 of that opinion.

In that case President Lincoln, or rather some of his supporters, raised a claim that since the Civil War was in progress that the military forces in Indiana had a right to try for treason, a man whom they called a Copperhead in those days because he was sympathetic toward the South. He was a civilian who had no connection with the military forces. So they set up a military commission and tried this man, a civilian, in a military court, and sentenced him to death.

One of the greatest lawyers this nation ever produced, Jeremiah Black, brought the battle to the Supreme Court and he told in his argument, which is one of the greatest arguments of all time, how the Constitution of the United States came into being. He said that the people who drafted and ratified that Constitution were determined that not one drop of the blood which had been shed throughout the ages to wrest power from arbitrary authority should be lost. So they went through all of the great documents of the English law from Magna Carta on down, and whatever they found there they incorporated in the Constitution to preserve the liberties of the people.

Now although the Constitution gave a civilian the right to trial in civilian courts, and the right to be indicted by a grand jury before he could be put on trial and then a right to be tried before a petit jury, the government argued that the president had the inherent power to suspend those constitutional principles because of the great emergency which existed at that time when the country was torn apart in the civil strife.

The Supreme Court of the United States rejected the argument that the president had any inherent power to ignore or suspend any of the guarantees of the Constitution, and Judge David Davis said, in effect: "The good and wise men who drafted and ratified the Constitution foresaw that troublous times would arise, when rulers and people would become restive under restraint and seek by sharp and decisive measures to accomplish ends deemed just and proper, and that the principles of Constitutional liberty would be put in peril unless established by irrepealable law."

Then he proceeded to say: "And for these reasons, these good and wise men drafted and ratified the Constitution as a law for rulers and people alike, at all times and under all circumstances."

Then he laid down this great statement: "No doctrine involving more pernicious consequences was ever invented by the wit of man than that any of its provisions can be suspended during any of the great exigencies of government."

And notwithstanding that, we have it argued here in this year of our Lord 1973 that the President of the United States has a right to suspend the Fourth Amendment and to have burglary committed just because he claims, or somebody acting for him claims, that the records of a psychiatrist about the emotional and mental state of his patient, Ellsberg, had some relation to national security.

Now, President Nixon himself defined the national security

in one of his directives as including only two things: national
defense, and relations with foreign countries. How in the world
opinions of a psychiatrist about the mental state or the emotional state or the psychological state of his patient, even if his
patient was Ellsberg, could have any relation to national
defense or relations to a foreign country is something which
eludes the imagination of this country lawyer.

჻ Between the Fielding burglary on September 3, 1971, and the
beginning of the Senate Select Committee hearing on May 17, 1973,
to wit, in April, 1973, Ellsberg was placed on trial before United
States District Judge W. Matthew Byrne and a jury on the criminal
charge arising against him in respect to the Pentagon Papers in the
district court sitting in California.

During the pendency of the trial, the Department of Justice discovered that the Fielding burglary had been committed, and despite
President Nixon's reluctance, the department communicated that
fact to Judge Byrne, who forthwith inquired of it whether Ellsberg's
telephone had been wiretapped also.

After so doing, Judge Byrne publicly disclosed that at the request
of the White House he had met with Ehrlichman on April 5 and 7
during the pendency of the Ellsberg case, and Ehrlichman had
indicated to him that the President was considering him for appointment as permanent director of the FBI.

Pursuant to Judge Byrne's inquiry, the acting director of the FBI,
William D. Ruckelshaus, a public servant of the highest honor,
investigated and discovered these facts: The FBI had wiretapped
Ellsberg; the logs of the wiretaps had disappeared from the FBI
files; and their whereabouts were unknown to the FBI.

Upon receipt of this information, Judge Byrne dismissed the
charges against Ellsberg because his constitutional rights had been
violated.

Shortly after this event, it was ascertained that the logs of Ellsberg's wiretaps had been removed from the FBI and stored in a safe
in the White House office that Ehrlichman had occupied.

჻ Friday, July 13, 1973, was an unlucky day for President Nixon.
On that day, Alexander Butterfield, a former White House aide who

was then chief of the Civil Aeronautics Board, made dramatic revelations to the staff of the Senate committee. He told the staff that President Nixon had secretly recorded on voice-activated tape recorders all conversations he had with others in the Oval Office of the White House and his office in the Executive Office Building since early 1971. The tapes recording these conversations were in the custody of the Secret Service agents assigned to the White House, he continued, and these tapes would disclose whether John Dean, the former counsel to the President, had testified truthfully or lied when he told the Senate committee that the President had aided and abetted some of his aides in concealing from law enforcement officers, the press, and the people the truth about the misconduct of his aides during the presidential election of 1972 and the Watergate burglary.

The committee forthwith requested President Nixon to make five tapes recording his secret conversations with John Dean available to it. While he asserted the tapes would exonerate him from any wrongdoing, President Nixon refused this request. In so doing, he manifested his unrelenting purpose to thwart the committee's efforts to ascertain the truth concerning the matters it was authorized to investigate.

The committee thereupon subpoenaed Alfred C. Wong, the Secret Service agent allegedly in charge of the tapes it was seeking, to appear before Senator Baker and me for interrogation in an executive session. When Wong appeared before us, he was accompanied by the general counsel of the Department of the Treasury, which has jurisdiction over Secret Service agents. The general counsel handed us a letter dated the previous day which President Nixon had written the secretary of the Treasury, George P. Schultz. The letter ordered that no officer or agent of the Secret Service should give the committee "any testimony concerning matters observed or learned . . . while performing their duties at the White House."

In obedience to the President's order, Wong refused to testify, and the committee decided it would be unjust for it to ask that he be adjudged guilty of contempt for obeying the President.

During a committee hearing two days later, I received a telephone call from a man who professed to be Secretary Schultz and who advised me that President Nixon had decided to make available to the committee tapes of conversations with witnesses before it relevant to the matters the committee was authorized to investigate and that President Nixon would meet with me as chairman of the committee during the next week to establish procedures by which this could be done. I was delighted to receive this information, and forthwith advised the committee and the audience in open session as to what Secretary Schultz had told me.

Shortly afterward, I received assurances from Secretary Schultz that he had had no telephone conversation with me, and that some-one had obviously impersonated him. On learning that I had been the victim of a prankster, I made a statement with amusement to the committee and audience in open session.

As I recollect my remarks, I said, "It appears that a hoax has been perpetrated on the chairman of the committee. I have just had a con-versation with a man who assured me that he is the real Secretary Schultz, that he has had no telephonic conversation with me today, and that whoever did was somebody else. It is an awful thing for a trusting soul like me to find that there are human beings, if you can call them such, who would perpetrate a hoax like this. I trust that nobody in the future will attempt to deceive and mislead a trusting and unsuspicious individual like the chairman of this committee in any such fashion. Counsel suggests we have had some talk about dirty tricks. I think it is the unanimous opinion of this committee that this is a right dirty trick."

༄ At times the committee and its members were harassed by events more troublesome than this prank. On several occasions the committee received notice that bombs had been planted in the Sen-ate Caucus Room, where the hearings were held, and the police searched for them with explosive-sniffing dogs and thus ascertained that the information came from pranksters.

I received many furtive threats on my life, and while I never dis-cussed the matter with them, I am satisfied that the other members of the committee had similar experiences.

The Capitol Hill Police fielded many of the threats against me. In their concern, they wanted to provide me plain-clothes bodyguards for all hours of the day. I did accept the service of a police officer to help ease my way through the throng which packed the hallway between my office and the Senate Caucus Room, but I declined the service of a bodyguard on other occasions. As I told the police, I had long since decided I was not immortal, and believed that not even a legion of bodyguards could protect me from the pot shot of a crackpot.

Perhaps the meanest of these threats reached me at my apartment just as my wife and I were leaving for a reception given by some of our friends in celebration of our fiftieth wedding anniversary. If I dared to attend the reception, I was warned, I would be assassinated.

❦   A few incidents of this nature did have a humorous side. During the course of the hearings, I went to Cincinnati to deliver the commencement address at the University of Cincinnati. When I returned to my motel suite, I found two Cincinnati police officers awaiting me. Their chief, it seemed, had received a secretive call threatening my assassination. Consequently they were to spend the night in my suite and look after me while I was in Cincinnati. As one of them remarked, with true Irish wit, "I don't know how much the chief is concerned with your assassination. But I am absolutely convinced he doesn't want it to happen in Cincinnati."

❦   After Butterfield disclosed the existence of President Nixon's secret tapes, the committee and the special prosecutors, who had been appointed to prosecute criminal charges arising out of the Watergate affair, diligently sought in all available ways to require Nixon to make specified tapes available to them for evidential purposes. President Nixon, who must have known what the tapes contained respecting the allegations against him, strenuously resisted their efforts.

While so doing, he stated the tapes would exonerate him from any wrongdoing. Moreover, he repeatedly and positively assured the American people that he had no knowledge or information concerning the Watergate burglary before March, 1973, when John Dean indicated to him that some of his aides may have been involved in it and in subsequent efforts to cover it up. He assured the public from that time onward that he urged all executive officials and employees cognizant of all matters relevant to Watergate to reveal what they knew to law enforcement officers.

The ultimate effort of the Senate committee to obtain a judicial decree compelling Nixon to make the five tapes sought by it available to it was frustrated by the United States Court of Appeals for the District of Columbia in an adverse ruling which I maintain was constitutionally and legally indefensible. The committee was precluded from seeking a review of the ruling by the Supreme Court because the circuit court ignored the committee's request for expedited action and did not make its ruling until the committee's power to act was expiring under the resolution which created it.

Special prosecutors Archibald Cox and Leon Jaworski were successful, however, in their quest for the tapes they sought.

By a decree of the circuit court sought by Special Prosecutor Cox, President Nixon was ordered to produce before Judge John J. Sirica of the United States District Court of the District of Columbia tapes made on September 15, 1972, and in February, March, and April, 1973, which corroborated the testimony Dean had given the committee indicating Nixon's complicity in the cover-up of the misconduct of his offending aides and the Watergate burglary. The contents of these tapes were not publicly revealed, however, at the time.

By the unanimous ruling of the eight participating justices on an expedited appeal by Special Prosecutor Jaworski, which was handed down on July 24, 1974, President Nixon was required to produce before Judge Sirica a number of additional tapes, including three tapes of conversations of Nixon and his chief of staff, H. R. ("Bob") Haldeman, which occurred on June 23, 1972, just six days after the burglars were caught in the headquarters of the Democratic National Committee in the Watergate complex.

Nixon had apparently denied his own lawyers access to his secret tapes until just before the judicial decrees required their submission to Judge Sirica. This was undoubtedly true of the tapes of June 23, 1972. By their own words imprinted by their own voices on the three tapes of June 23, 1972, President Nixon and Bob Haldeman made it indisputable that they knew these things within six days after the Watergate burglary:

1. That the burglary was an operation of the committee Nixon had established to manage his campaign for reelection.

2. That the operation was financed by Nixon's campaign funds.

3. That the FBI suspected that the burglary was an operation of either the CIA or the White House.

4. That the FBI was on the verge of tracing to their sources the specific campaign funds that financed the burglary, and thus discovering that the burglary was an operation of Nixon's reelection committee.

5. That such a discovery was likely to imperil the political security of Nixon, and for that reason it was imperative that the threatened discovery be prevented.

The three tapes further revealed that Nixon and Haldeman agreed that the FBI could be persuaded to stop its investigation of this matter if the CIA would assure it that the investigation was about to uncover a covert operation of the CIA. The CIA could be induced to give the FBI this assurance if Haldeman and John D. Ehrlichman, Nixon's adviser on domestic affairs, with Nixon's approval, told Richard M. Helms and Vernon A. Walters, the director and deputy director of the CIA, that the FBI's further investigation of the matter would open up the entire Bay of Pigs episode and disastrously affect the nation's foreign policy. Pursuant to this agreement, the tapes showed, Haldeman and Ehrlichman forthwith contacted Helms and Walters and were satisfied that they would persuade the FBI to stop its investigation of this matter, and thus forestall the threatened political peril.

As Robert Burns said, "The best laid schemes of mice and men gang aft a-gley."

Haldeman erred in reporting to President Nixon that Helms and Walters would implement their agreement. Instead of doing so, they assured the FBI that the CIA was not involved in any way in the Watergate affair and that the FBI's continued investigation of the matter would not uncover any covert operation on its part.

When he listened to the tapes of June 23, 1972, preparatory to submitting them to Judge Sirica pursuant to the Supreme Court ruling, Fred Buzhardt, one of Nixon's lawyers, suffered consternation and is reputed to have said, "This ends everything—this is the smoking pistol."

The tapes affected General Alexander M. Haig, Jr., the White House chief of staff, and James D. St. Clair, Nixon's chief Watergate counsel, in like manner. Haig is reputed to have advised Vice-President Ford to be prepared to assume the presidency within a few days. St. Clair was outraged by these tapes. He had argued before courts on the basis of information given him by Nixon that his client was not implicated in the cover-up of the Watergate affair, and he demanded that Nixon give public assurances that he and his associates had never had access to them.

Nixon released these tapes to the public with a statement affirming, in essence, that he had forgotten the conversations they recorded. They had a devastating impact on his political fortunes. At the time of their release, the House Judiciary Committee had completed its impeachment hearings, and all of its members, except ten dissenting Republican congressmen, had voted to impeach President Nixon for obstruction of justice and other alleged offenses.

These tapes refuted the truth of the assurances of innocence Nixon had given the American people throughout the two preceding years. In conjunction with previously released tapes, they disclosed that he became implicated in efforts to hide the truth about Watergate as early as June 23, 1972, and persisted in such efforts from that time onward. It is not surprising that the Watergate grand jury named him an unindicted coconspirator.

In addition, they demolished testimony given the Senate committee by Haldeman and Ehrlichman that they had contacted Helms and Walters of the CIA simply because President Nixon honestly believed that the FBI was about to uncover a covert CIA operation and thus imperil the national security.

After the release of the tapes of June 23, 1972, the ten dissenting Republican congressmen publicly announced that the tapes showed that President Nixon had obstructed justice and that they would vote to impeach him on that ground when the House acted on the Judiciary Committee's recommendations.

Hugh Scott, the Republican leader of the Senate, John J. Rhodes, the Republican leader of the House, and Senator Barry Goldwater visited the White House and told Nixon, in effect, that his impeachment by the House and his conviction by the Senate were certain.

At noon on August 9, 1974, Nixon became the first president in history to resign the presidency, and Vice-President Ford qualified as his successor. On the evening of the preceding day Nixon had informed the American people in a televised speech of his purpose to resign and stated that he was prompted to do so solely because he no longer had "a strong enough basis in the Congress" to justify efforts to remain in office.

In the same speech, Nixon said, "I regret deeply any injuries that I may have done in the course of the events that led to my decision. I would say only that if some of my judgments were wrong—and some were wrong—they were made in what I believed at the time to be the best interest of the nation." These statements can scarcely be reconciled with the constitutional obligation that rested on Nixon as president to take care that the laws be faithfully executed.

The House Judiciary Committee filed with its parent body a 528-page report of its impeachment inquiry. When Nixon resigned, the House accepted the report and ended the impeachment proceeding without further action.

Many hard-core Nixon supporters maintain that Nixon did no evil in the Watergate affair, and that he was wrongly driven from the presidency by political partisans and a hostile news media. The ten Republican congressmen who voted against all impeachment proposals in the House Judiciary Committee emphatically deny the validity of these assertions in so-called minority views embodied in the committee's report. They stated in their minority views that "Richard Nixon, as President, committed certain acts for which he should have been impeached, and removed from office," and gave these reasons for their conclusion:

> We know that it has been said, and perhaps some will continue to say, that Richard Nixon was "hounded from office" by his political opponents and media critics. We feel constrained to point out, however, that it was Richard Nixon who impeded the FBI's investigation of the Watergate affair by wrongfully attempting to implicate the Central Intelligence Agency; it was Richard Nixon, who created and preserved the evidence of that transgression and who, knowing that it had been subpoenaed by this Committee and the Special Prosecutor, concealed its terrible import, even from his own counsel, until he could do so no longer. And it was a unanimous Supreme Court of the United States which, in an opinion authored by the Chief

Justice, whom he appointed, ordered Richard Nixon to surrender that evidence to the Special Prosecutor, to further the ends of justice.

The tragedy that finally engulfed Richard Nixon has many facets. One was the very self-inflicted nature of the harm. It is striking that such an able, experienced and perceptive man, whose ability to grasp the global implications of events little noticed by others may well have been unsurpassed by any of his predecessors, should fail to comprehend the damage that accrued daily to himself, his Administration, and to the Nation, as day after day, month after month, he imprisoned the truth about his role in the Watergate cover-up so long and so tightly within the solitude of his Oval Office that it could not be unleashed without destroying his Presidency.

A woman wrote me a letter in which she called me a "miserable wretch," charged I had helped to drive from office "the greatest President our nation ever had," and expressed the wish that I was "feeling as bad as I deserved to feel."

In response, I wrote her that her letter indicated I had a higher opinion of former president Nixon than she had. When he admitted, in substance, on the tapes of June 23, 1972, that he became engaged in the cover-up of the Watergate burglary six days after its commission, I believed he was telling the truth, and she evidently thought he was lying.

All in all, the Senate committee received about 1.5 million communications from Americans during its investigation of the Watergate affair. About sixty-five thousand of them condemned the investigation as a partisan "witch-hunt," and the remainder praised it as a patriotic service to the country.

Our grandson, Bobby Ervin, who was then about thirteen years of age, visited my wife and me in Washington during the Watergate investigation. We were walking to dinner at Mike Palm's Restaurant on Pennsylvania Avenue trailed by some reporters and news photographers. A reporter asked Bobby, "How does it feel to be going to dinner with the chairman of the Watergate Committee?" Bobby replied, "It's like going to the circus with the organ grinder."

Finale

As a finale, I end what I say about humor with the last words of the character who gave his name to Irving Bacheller's book *Eben Holden: A Tale of the North Country*:

> I ain't afraid.
> 'Shamed o' nuthin' I ever done.
> Alwuss kep' my tugs tight,
> Never swore 'less 'twas nec'sary,
> Never ketched a fish bigger'n 't was
> Er lied 'n a hoss trade
> Er shed a tear I didn't hev to.
> Never cheated anybody but Eben Holden.
> Goin' off somewheres, Bill—dunno the way nuther—
> Dunno 'f it's east er west er north er south,
> Er road er trail;
> But I ain't afraid.

Index